Praise for
The Edible Ecosystem Solution

Zach Loeks uses a rich palette of strategies and species that make sense in his region, to inspire people everywhere to create an edible ecosystem in theirs, and so become more connected to and nourished by nature. This richly illustrated book brings the permaculture vision of a recreated Garden of Eden to new audiences ready to dive into their own edible ecosystems.

—DAVID HOLMGREN, co-originator of permaculture

For most of human existence we learned to live by hunting and gathering from nature's abundance and generosity. Agriculture marked a fundamental shift in how we lived. Now, COVID-19 confronts us with how destructive and frail our globalized industrial food system has become. Resilience in an increasingly uncertain future demands that most of our food must be grown locally. In taking an ecological approach to growing our own plants for consumption, Zach Loeks provides an approach that will be vital in a warming world.

—DAVID SUZUKI, award-winning geneticist, author, and broadcaster

It's easy to think we could simply shift from polluting and strictly ornamental landscaping habits to ones that produce food and wildlife habitat, and with no greater level of thought, instantly return to paradise. Instead, this book is inviting us to the task of re-weaving ourselves and our communities into the web of life.

—JASON GERHARDT, regenerative designer, Real Earth Design

Zach Loeks has the uncanny ability to deep-dive visually in his writing for specific aspects of permaculture in a way that only a second generation permaculturist can. From his stunning illustrations, to his clear and engaging writing style, to his regenerative and inspiring meta-solutions, Zach has done it again!

—MATT POWERS, ThePermacultureStudent.com

Loeks invites us to take back our green spaces and convert them from simple places of ornamentation to a practical source of food for our families and communities and thereby transform our future, garden plot by garden plot.

—CATALINA MARGULIS, *Harrowsmith Magazine*

Zach Loeks makes a compelling case for edible ecosystems and shows the ways in which our schools, colleges and universities can play a central role in this change. I can strongly recommend this book.

—ALAN NASH, Professor, Department of Geography, Planning and Environment, Concordia University

Zach lays out a beautiful path to transform our homes and communities with edible ecosystems that improves our quality of life, creates food security, and increases biodiversity for the species we share our homes with. If every human who feels deep down that we need a new path forward used this guide, we could find ourselves in an ecological revolution.

—Rob Greenfield, environmental activist, author,
Food Freedom and *Dude Making a Difference*

Our ancestors survived and thrived along ecological edges of edible abundance. Modern civilization has plowed and paved over biodiversity leaving impoverished landscapes. In *The Edible Ecosystem Solution*, author Zach Loeks provides tools and insights to restore edible abundance, resilience, and security to individual yards, community spaces, rural landscapes, and collectively, the world.

—Thomas J. Elpel, author, *Botany in a Day* and *Green Prosperity*

A great handbook to help you create a complete edible garden ecosystem by turning a small part of your yard into a veritable hotspot of biological diversity, regeneration, and culinary joy. *The Edible Ecosystem Solution* successfully preaches how to spread the benefits of your garden throughout your neighborhood and even the world.

—Jeff Lowenfels, Lord of the Roots, author,
the *Teaming Trilogy* and *DIY Autoflowering Cannabis*

Educate, Propagate, Inspire, indeed! *The Edible Ecosystem Solution* is at once a work of art and a valuable tool in our journey towards an ecological society. Zach Loeks' rich illustrations and creative design breaks new ground in conveying permaculture concepts to the reader. His deep research and clear presentation inspire the reader to rediscover our ancient roots as ecosystem managers. I will certainly be adding this book to my permaculture design course reading list!

—Darrell E. Frey, Three Sisters Farm, author,
Bioshelter Market Garden, co-author, *The Food Forest Handbook*

Where most people see lots, grass, or property lines, Zach Loeks sees the potential for dynamic edible ecosystems, ones that can transform our cities and neighborhoods into regenerating, life-giving, health-giving natural bonanzas. Here is his primer and his blueprint for starting small and thinking big.

—Florence Williams, author, *The Nature Fix*

A beautifully-illustrated and approachable formula for creating abundance.

—Michelle Avis, Verge Permaculture, co-author, *Essential Rainwater Harvesting*

THE **EDIBLE ECOSYSTEM** SOLUTION

Growing BIODIVERSITY in Your Backyard and Beyond

ZACH LOEKS

WITH
300 ILLUSTRATIONS AND DESIGNS
BY THE AUTHOR

new society
PUBLISHERS

Cover design by Diane McIntosh.

Printed in Canada. First printing November 2020.

Inquiries regarding requests to reprint all or part of *The Edible Ecosystem Solution* should be addressed to New Society Publishers at the address below. To order directly from the publishers, please call toll-free (North America) 1-800-567-6772, or order online at newsociety.com

Any other inquiries can be directed by mail to:
New Society Publishers
P.O. Box 189, Gabriola Island, BC V0R 1X0, Canada
(250) 247-9737

LIBRARY AND ARCHIVES CANADA CATALOGUING IN PUBLICATION

Title: The edible ecosystem solution : growing biodiversity in your backyard and beyond / Zach Loeks ; with 300 illustrations and designs by the author.

Names: Loeks, Zach, 1985- author, illustrator.

Description: Includes bibliographical references and index.

Identifiers: Canadiana (print) 20200303821 | Canadiana (ebook) 20200303910 | ISBN 9780865719347 (softcover) | ISBN 9781550927276 (PDF) | ISBN 9781771423236 (EPUB)

Subjects: LCSH: Permaculture. | LCSH: Edible landscaping. | LCSH: Gardens—Design. | LCSH: Human ecology.

Classification: LCC S494.5.P47 L59 2020 | DDC 631.5/8—dc23

Canada

New Society Publishers' mission is to publish books that contribute in fundamental ways to building an ecologically sustainable and just society, and to do so with the least possible impact on the environment, in a manner that models this vision.

Dedication

This book is for anyone who has ever planted a plant, enjoyed a berry, or wondered what they could do to build better community and a more resilient world. If this book results in encouraging a reader to plant a single food plant guild, it has succeeded. If it results in the new gardener sharing their experience with neighbors who then plant a single food plant guild, it has contributed to a peaceful revolution.

For my own little companion planting: Vera, Alex, Dayvah, and Rainah, and for the generations of family who have supported my work: the city planner, artist, agronomist, community activist, avid gardener, educator, designer, and teacher.

For the team at New Society Publishers for their great work, support in this vision, and all the nitty-gritty. Thank you!

With love and appreciation to all those who work to grow healthy and resilient communities and support this work through their stewardship here, there, and everywhere.

Zach Loeks

So here we go, back and to the future, one spot at a time, one page at a time, together.

Thesis

When I first started writing this book, I was focused on why people should **maximize their yards with gardens and edible landscapes**. More specifically, I wanted to teach people how to turn a single piece of lawn into a garden and show how straightforward and affordable this actually can be. One small area, no greater than 25 square feet—essentially, a garden *spot*—is a great starting point for creating more garden abundance in your yard, along with all the benefits it can provide to your well-being. The book is about *this* and much more.

I have always been intrigued by ecosystems, whether woodlands, meadows, or the vast prairies that used to stretch across North America. If you are like me, an ecosystem becomes so much richer when it is edible and useful, such as fruit and nut forests, berry meadows, or prairies full of medicinally useful plants.

And the concept of the **micro-ecosystem**! It's a rich idea that an entire ecosystem can be found within a small space. **An entire ecosystem in just 25 square feet**. Imagine! And, when you plant an edible ecosystem, all the benefits of the landscape-scale ecosystem also exist within your micro-landscape. We should be planting more than just gardens. We should be planting edible ecosystems! These provide fresh fruits, berries, and herbs, as well as societal services like air, water, and soil production and purification. Ecosystem landscapes are spaces of rejuvenation, community well-being, and life support, and every spot can contribute directly, right where we live. They even serve to enrich a microscopic ecosystem—inside us! We are living ecological beings.

After all, human existence is a story of living surrounded by **diverse, edible, and useful ecosystems.** Our minds, bodies, and nervous systems evolved within ancestral, wild ecosystems, and we still benefit from their goods and services. Biodiversity is well-known to have been key to human success and remains so for modern societal resilience. A garden can be designed as a piece of true human habitat.

A small garden is something anyone, anywhere, can get growing; and together, these many small spots would create **immense ecosystem services for society**. All the skills needed for gardening success could be extrapolated from a single spot—to fill a yard, a community, or beyond. This is a modular way of inspiring and acting for greater change. There is beauty in the simplicity of small beginnings—transitioning one spot and then leveraging it to assist in the transition of more community spaces. After all, there is so much underutilized greenspace in our communities that is ready for ecological abundance.

Consider how everyday people can make positive community change in this approachable and achievable manner. Envision your community, and put a foot down on one spot of yard to get going. Your little spot's possibilities are endless: from berries, fruits, and herbs to pollinator habitat and flowers for beekeeping; from new shade trees with abundant mulberries to native prairie restoration and agrobiodiversity conservation. These settings are points of conservation and conversation, places of ethics and activism, and spaces of sanctuary and healing—one bit of ecosystem to stand tall in the face of the degradation of **our wild ancestral landscapes** and upholding the resilience of our society in these uncertain times. Our beginnings could have far-reaching edible ecological ripples with a bit of **inspiration, education, and plant propagation**.

This book, *The Edible Ecosystem Solution*, is about designing edible micro-landscapes that serve to enrich your life, but they are also starting points for immense **community land transition.** By transitioning land in our communities, **people change**. When people are surrounded by the sights, smells, flavors, textures, and experiences of our ancestral world, there is a subtle and powerful shift in the community. **When people change, our culture is transformed**. We begin to find profit from the land, building a truly green economy—from the ground up. We understand ecosystem goods and services and support them directly through **stewardship**. We orient around the seasons and celebrate their bounty and plan for their scarcity. We are healthy, happy, and productive. **We become an ecosystem culture**.

An ecosystem culture is one that benefits from—and supports—its diverse, edible, and useful abundance. Decisions are made and policy-making is done from this point of view. And throughout all walks of society, we

The Ecosystem Solution Institute is dedicated to Education, Propagation, and Inspiration for the transition of landscapes to edible biodiversity and ecosystem benefits. Learn more at www. ecosystemsolutioninstitute.com and @ZachLoeks on social media.

honor diversity and conserve and nurture it as an **immense repository of wealth, resilience, and well-being**. We prioritize edible, diverse abundance in communities as a **human right**. Our societies prosper not on the finite resources of the land but within healthy, regenerative ecosystems.

Is it a stretch to think that this can all happen from simply planting an edible ecosystem garden in your yard? I don't think so. We know that natural principles are a force to be reckoned with, and one of the most fundamental principles is that of **dispersal**. Ecosystems expand naturally to fill land when they are successful, and humans are a powerful force for dispersal of useful diversity. Like a dandelion blowing in the wind, we can transition land, change people, and transform culture—one location at a time.

The EPI System presented in this book is about catalyzing the potential of a single garden to transform our planet. In many ways, this book is more about the psychology of change than the "how-to" of edible landscape design. We all want a piece of edible Eden, and a single yard has the potential to be a source point for change. And many gardens, with many stewards, make big benefits for society! This book examines human origins and **ecosystem benefits**, reveals **modern opportunities** for land transition, and outlines a **step-by-step plan** for building a single, edible ecosystem with the capacity to **catalyze land transition** in communities for societal wealth, well-being, and resilience.

About This Book

The design of this book maximizes illustrations, infographics, and photos to move the conversation forward. It also makes use of colors to inform readers and clarify the discussion. For instance, to clarify the relationship between different food plants in a garden, they are assigned a color. Just as the primary colors blend to make secondary colors, the relationships of Earth's biodiversity combine for human well-being and societal resilience. This book starts in space, with the Earth as a distinct object and then proceeds to unfold the story and information as we zoom into our human habitat: Earth, our yards, and single garden spot! I hope that you enjoy *experiencing* this book. It was a pleasure illustrating, writing, and photographing it to be immersive.

"Unless someone like you cares a whole awful lot,
Nothing is going to get better. It's not."

— Dr. Seuss, *The Lorax*

Illustrated Outline

**Section 1
The Ecology of
Humanity**

**Section 2
Solutions and
Opportunities**

**Section 5
Ecosystem Culture**

**Section 3
Edible Ecosystem
Design**

**Section 4
Educate, Propagate,
Inspire**

Contents

Section 5: Ecosystem Culture

The Ecology of Humanity

OUR EARTH IS A UNIQUE PLACE IN SPACE not just because it possesses a cosmic blend of elements that make it inhabitable, but because it is our home. Of all the planets in the universe, we live here! Earth is precious! Surrounded by the immense unknown of the universe, still mostly incomprehensible to human minds, our Earth is a habitable, enjoyable, incredible place in space. The Earth is over 4.3 billion years old. Our species, *Homo sapiens*, have evolved for the last 200,000 years, and our genus *Homo* emerged on this planet over 2 million years ago. We have primarily inhabited areas of diverse useful and edible abundance—edible ecosystems were our habitat, and they are a cornerstone of societal success and human well-being. This first chapter is a gradual introduction to knowledge about our natural systems and our place within ecosystems.

Precious Place in Space

Let's take a look at our little Earth—
a unique environmental blend that supports life.

A Rare Opportunity

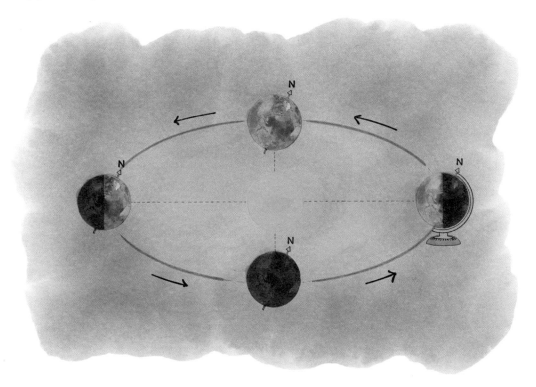

What a precious place…this Earth of ours. It is a rare opportunity to have a planet as livable as ours. Mars is too cold and arid, and Venus is too hot. From the tilt of our axis to the proximity to the sun and the magnetic field around us, our Earth is unique in our solar system and universally rare. It is a life-giving environment.

The tilt of Earth's axis and its orbits around the sun provide our seasons.

Environmental Spheres

Our planet is composed of **three environmental (or physical) spheres**: atmosphere (air and gases), lithosphere (minerals and rocks), and hydrosphere (water).

These environmental conditions react with the sun's energy, which radiates through space and into our atmosphere. The sun's heat is absorbed by oceans and land, warming our planet and creating the spark of life. These spheres are part of **Earth's life-support system**. Without solar energy, gravity, and the cycling of nutrients, there would be no life on Earth. Biological diversity has flourished over Earth's surface, in its oceans, and its air. What an amazing thing, this spark of life and the diversity that has evolved!

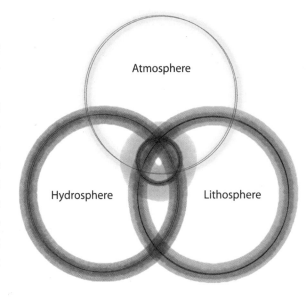

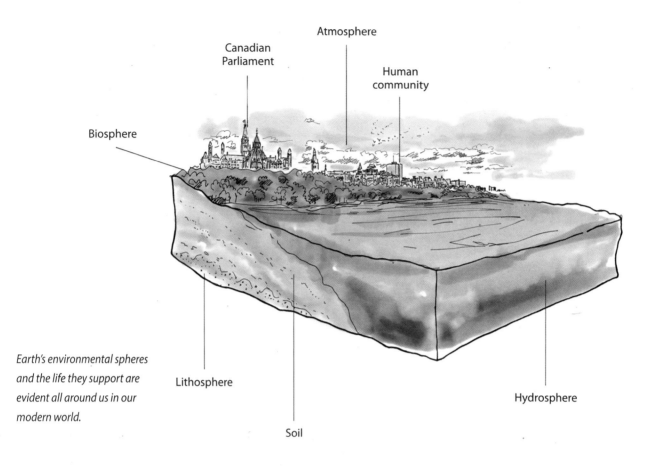

Earth's environmental spheres and the life they support are evident all around us in our modern world.

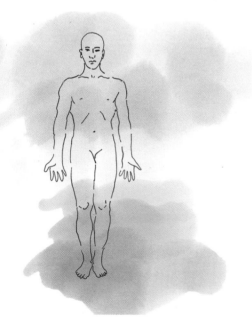

Elemental Human

These same elements that make our planet habitable can be found within the human body. Our bodies are made of minerals: our bones and teeth are mostly calcium, and iron is in our blood; there is air in our lungs, water in our tissues and organs, and electricity in our nervous system. We are made of the stuff of the Earth. Humans are a part of the environment, and conservation of Earth's systems is protection of our well-being.

Biodiversity

Come in closer, let's see this planet of ours! *We occupy a unique zone on planet Earth, shared with an abundance of biodiversity on which we depend.*

Biosphere

The **biosphere** is the sum total of life on Earth: every creature, every microorganism, and every tree, bee and butterfly. The biosphere is the fourth sphere in which life can exist, and it only occurs within a narrow band along the Earth's surface.

Life Zone

Life only exists within a band called the **life zone**. If the Earth were a basketball, this life zone would only be as thick as the skin of the ball. We need to protect and regenerate the life systems that exist within this narrow zone. With thousands of miles of uninhabited rock beneath our feet and an unlivable atmosphere above us, this is the space that is *just right*. Here, the three bears, Goldilocks, and all the rest of the Earth's estimated 2 billion species[1] find space to live. The life zone contains habitat for humans, lichen, beasts and birds, fish and fowl, plants and trees, microbes, and fungi.

Biomes

This amazingly habitable planet has **ten major ecological systems (*biomes*)** that occur within the Earth's biosphere. Biomes are vast areas with distinctly similar plants, animals, and other life forms that have adapted to unique environments. Earth's variability in climate, terrain, and water produces unique conditions for the evolution of life adapted to these regional differences. For this reason, you will see succulent plants in all desert areas, though some are endemic to the Gobi and others to the Kalahari.

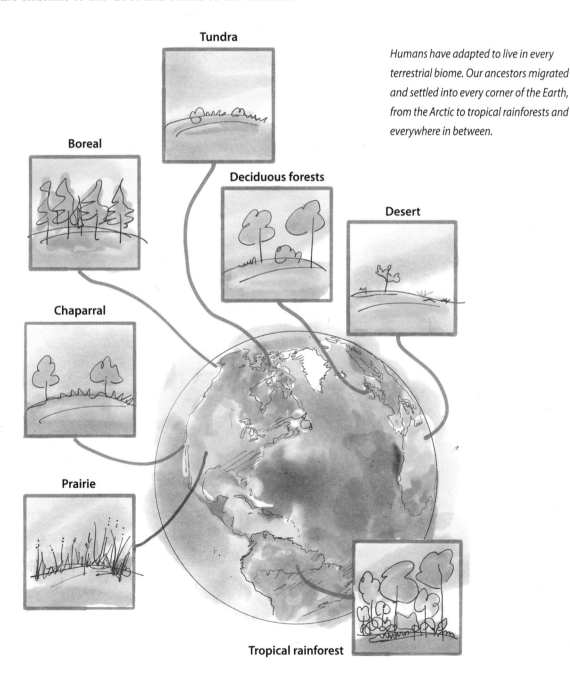

Humans have adapted to live in every terrestrial biome. Our ancestors migrated and settled into every corner of the Earth, from the Arctic to tropical rainforests and everywhere in between.

Organization of Life

Life on Earth is understood by science as fitting into different categories; this is called the **organization of life**. Biomes are the broadest category of life on Earth after the biosphere itself. You are an **individual** and part of a **population** of humans (*Homo sapiens*). We all live within a **community** of different living organisms, such as foxes, deer, birds and trees, and grass. Each community is part of a particular **ecosystem**, meaning a community of living organisms that interact with each other and their non-living environment. There are many sorts of ecosystems within a biome.

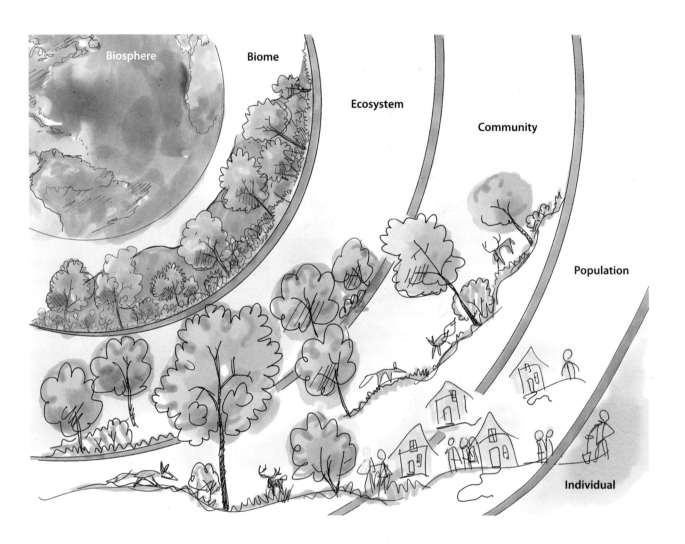

Biodiversity

Biodiversity is the variety and abundance of life.

We can consider biodiversity as being three-fold: **species**, **genes**, and **ecosystems.** In other words, there can be many different **species** of bees (bumble, honey, mason) in a meadow. The population of bumblebees in this meadow is composed of many individuals. Each individual has a unique **genetic variability**. These three different bee populations are part of a community of other organisms (birds, butterflies, frogs) in this meadow ecosystem. Each of these species is adding to the species richness of this ecosystem. This meadow is one of many ecosystems (woodland, wetland, etc.) that occur throughout a deciduous biome.

Honey bee   Mason bee   Bumble bee

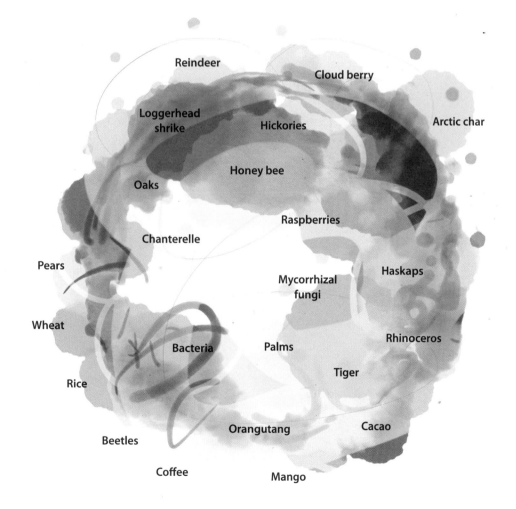

Reindeer
Cloud berry
Loggerhead shrike
Hickories
Arctic char
Honey bee
Oaks
Raspberries
Chanterelle
Pears
Haskaps
Mycorrhizal fungi
Wheat
Rhinoceros
Bacteria
Palms
Tiger
Rice
Orangutang
Cacao
Beetles
Coffee
Mango

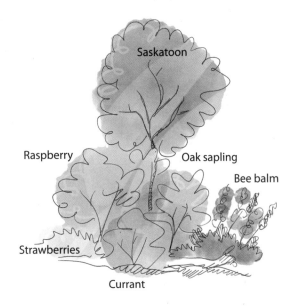

Species Richness Is Productive

Species-rich landscapes are particularly productive. Two landscapes with similar access to sun, soil, and comparable terrain, but a difference in species diversity will have different productivity, with increases in favor of the diversified landscape. This is because diverse organisms partition resources and create companionships. There is more **net primary productivity** (a measure of photosynthesis production in biomass) in **layered ecosystems** (woodland) than there is in a **single-species system** (wheat field or lawn).

Biodiversity Hot Spots

Some areas on Earth have particularly high biodiversity. Other regions have high biodiversity and also high **endemic diversity**, with species that occur nowhere else. And some have especially high *edible and useful diversity* for humans. Within any biome, areas of diversity richness can occur, and these are worth treasuring and marking for conservation and restoration efforts. Biodiversity has been a cornerstone for societal success and is one of the greatest allies we have for a future of wealth and wellness. It is important to note that these diversity-rich areas can occur as micro-ecosystems anywhere! They might be found in your backyard or in an abandoned industrial lot. Because human communities have been built in areas of high diversity, *some of the most important ecological resources are close-to-home*, and they demand our attention before they are lost. These are also proximate to us for maximum services to society when restored.

These are some of the most biodiverse areas on the planet. They are known as biodiversity "hot spots."

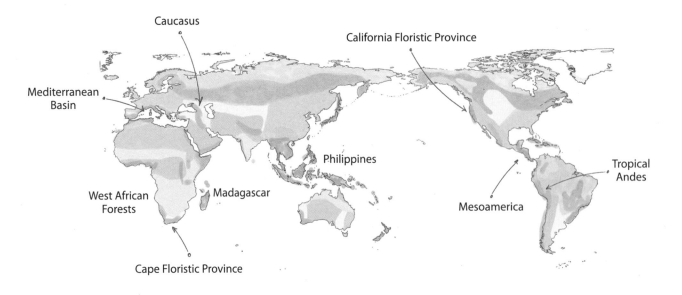

Ecosystems

Let's go closer. *North America, like all other continents, is a blend of ecological landscapes, or ecosystems, that support and are supported by biodiversity. Humans have made their home within all these ecosystems and have been supported by their biodiversity.*

What Is an Ecosystem?

An ecosystem is defined by dynamic interactions between **living** (biotic) organisms with each other and with their **non-living** (abiotic) environment. Humans can be part of an ecosystem. We constantly interact with other organisms, such as trees, foxes, and fungi, and certainly with each other. Our interactions with edible and useful plants, animals, and other life forms are of particular importance. Humans have always been connected to **edible and useful biodiversity**.

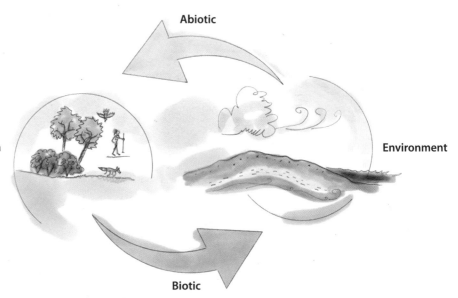

Ecosystems consist of organisms: animals, people, soil bacteria, etc., interacting with their environment (sun, water, air, minerals) and each other.

Ecosystem variations emerge where environmental differences within a biome's landscape occur. Due to subtle **micro-environmental** changes in a biome (moisture, terrain, soil, etc.), there are variations in plant and animal diversity composition. In a deciduous biome, a dragonfly could fly over three distinct ecosystems: meadow, wetland, and woodland. As we shall see in this book, the site-suitability of ecosystems to their environment is an important consideration in re-envisioning how humans design their landscape to work within **environmental constraints** and provide the benefits of different ecosystems.

Three ecosystems shown in a cross-section of a deciduous biome.

Ecological Succession

To understand ecological **succession,** picture the barren rock and pebble landscape left after the retreat of the glaciers at the end of the last glaciation here in the Northern Hemisphere (18,000 to 10,000 years ago). This rocky ground was slowly colonized by life. First came lichens, mosses, and then perennial herbs and grasses, followed by shrubs and sun-loving trees. Eventually, shade-tolerant tree species germinated and grew up to become part of a mature woodland ecosystem.

Our modern landscape is in a **stagnation of succession**; we spend a lot of money and energy fighting the natural phenomena of ecological succession, which provides us with benefits, as we shall discuss later on. Land planning that includes space for maturing our land use as evolving ecosystems will enjoy various benefits such as carbon capture, genetic resources, and water purification.

Successional Stages

Pioneer plants | Perennial plants and pioneer trees | Young woodland | Maturing forest

Succession

Time

A mosaic landscape of different successional stages maximizes biodiversity and other ecosystem benefits.

Here, we see a woodland, riparian, and prairie ecosystem meeting. This edge environment is very abundant.

The Productivity Between

Ecosystems in the intermediate stage of succession are very productive. The edges between different ecosystems at different stages of ecological succession are even more productive. Remember, **diversity is productivity**. So, a resilient and productive landscape is one with multiple types of ecosystems, with high species richness, at different stages of succession, and adjacent to each other. This is one of **nature's key lessons** that we can apply to land-use planning. If we redesign our cities, suburbs, and farms to include more diversity of ecosystems, and if we stagger their successional stages and improve the species richness of these landscapes, we create strong foundations for societal resilience in the face of disasters.

Ecosystem Form

Ecosystems have organisms with different forms (size and shape). For instance, in a woodland ecosystem, the plants have a variety of growth habits. Some grow tall, some creep along the ground, some climb, and some trees grow so high as to almost touch the sky. The form of a woodland ecosystem is easy to identify: it is well layered, and, in its mature state, the trees are large.

The same layering of different shapes also appears in a prairie ecosystem. Here, some grasses (such as big bluestem) can reach six feet tall; some are only a few inches high. The layering in the prairie is even more evident *within the soil* because some plant roots can grow 30 feet down.

Understanding the form of an ecosystem is important for maximizing land use in modern society. As we have already seen, a well-layered ecosystem is more productive. Integrating diverse layers in our farms and communities has benefits for humans that include increased carbon sequestration* to mitigate climate change and higher yields of desirable products like fruit or wood.

* Carbon sequestration is the removal of carbon from our atmosphere through the photosynthesis of living plants and its storage in their trunks, branches, roots, and the soil.

Tallgrass prairie ecosystems are diverse and layered ecological landscapes. Note: This sketch is an illustrated copy from an interpretive panel at the Tallgrass Prairie National Preserve, Kansas, and clearly illustrates the depth and shape of diverse prairie plants.

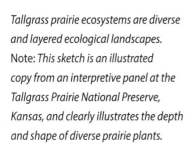

Ecological Function

The plants, animals, and other organisms in an ecosystem have roles to play for their own life cycles and for the system as a whole. For instance, plants with prolific flowers in spring attract pollinators, which are then nearby when fruit trees need pollination in early summer. It is said that form follows function. Certainly, the different shapes of plants in a woodland ecosystem are indicative of function. For instance, plants that creep on the ground help stabilize soils to the benefit of the whole system. The result of a diverse system is more potential benefits for all creatures in a given community.

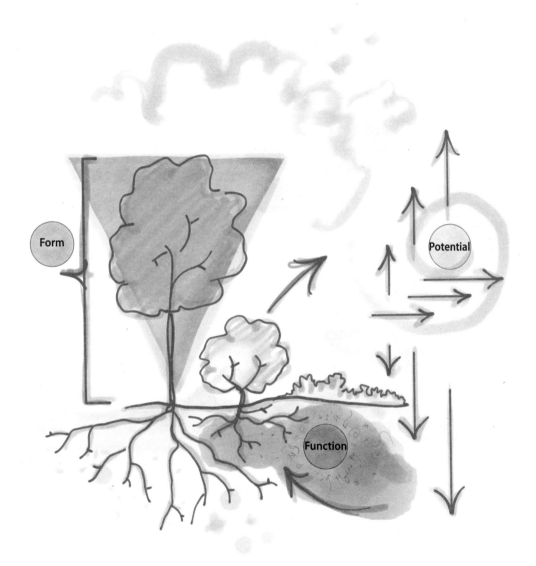

Ecosystem Services

Ecosystems have a multitude of benefits for humans; these can be thought of as ecosystem *goods* (resources) and *services*, or just the catch-all *ecosystem services*. Goods include products like fresh fruit, air, and kindling. Services include how ecosystems manage Earth's life-support systems, purification of water, soil building, sustaining biodiversity, etc.

Whole-System Potential

As a whole, ecosystems have tremendous potential. As time passes, they literally *build* potential, meaning there is more to go around for individual organisms, including humans, and they store potential that can be transferred to future productivity. Examples of ecosystem potential are the variety of seeds stored in a soil's seed bank, the buildup of organic matter in the soil, and the accumulation of carbon sequestered in the trees.

Consider the potential of a single tree. When an almond seed waits to germinate, it has its whole life ahead of it. As an oak seedling emerges, it is vulnerable; many growing together means some will survive. As a pear tree grows strong, it can offer more and more to the ecosystem as a whole. It has so much to offer humans, too. A maturing ecosystem can initially offer us berries and kindling; then it might provide fruit, nuts, and shade, and finally, it would yield lumber, medicinal and edible mushrooms, and copious seeds for future tree planting. While a young tree can bear only a handful of pears, a mature pear tree might bear 300 pounds of pears. *From one seed comes this pear tree that has the potential to produce 30,000 seeds.* Of those thousands of seedlings, only a few become old-growth trees, which is why we have only a few heritage trees left.

The depth of soil that was built by the prairie ecosystems of North America is another example of whole-system potential. The deep soils had a high capacity to hold water through droughts and provided great nutrient exchange. It was a productive ecosystem and habitat for many useful animal species, such as the bison. This ecosystem was very beneficial to humans for the last 10,000 years.

It is, tragically, almost gone. Because it was so productive, it was quickly turned into farms in the 19th and 20th centuries for **short-term agricultural gain**. However, this is resulting in **long-term pain** for our society because

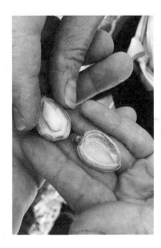

Soil organic matter is one of the most incredible results of mature ecosystems. It has immense potential to improve crop yields while helping mitigate climate change and other natural disasters.

we have literally eroded this amazing resource and are no longer benefiting from prairie ecosystem services. Returning the corn and grain belts of North America to a mix of regenerative farming and ecosystem restoration can help reverse climate change and improve farm productivity by recapturing carbon and putting it back into our soil, and using it to improve yields.

This prairie ecosystem has high species richness. The diverse plants have different forms and functions and provide habitat for many grassland birds, butterflies, and bees. It was also home to one of the most important species for human society to ever roam the Earth: the bison. The ecological potential of the prairies is their deep, rich topsoil, which is now being farmed across Canada and the United States. As such, there is less than 1% of the original tallgrass prairie left. This current land use is not building potential; it is mining, as a finite resource, the product of a once-regenerative system.

What Is an Edible Ecosystem?

An edible ecosystem is like any ecosystem, except it has more edible and useful plants. Edible ecosystems can be wild, or they can be designed and planted by humans. Sometimes, an edible ecosystem is right under our nose, and we just have to recognize what is already there. And sometimes it requires the purposeful cultivation of a food forest, with plants chosen for their usefulness to humans.

A forest is an ecosystem; a fruit forest is an edible ecosystem.

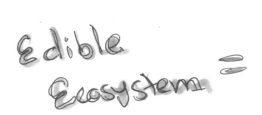  

An edible ecosystem has a diversity of edible and useful plants for humanity. Humans have always been drawn to edible diversity, orientating our internal compass to true food north.

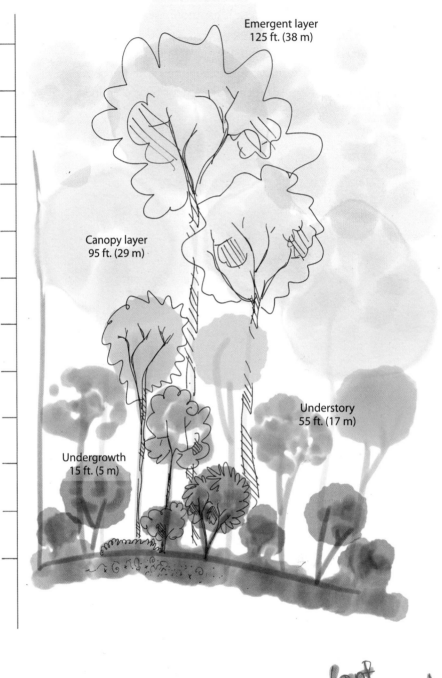

Emergent layer
125 ft. (38 m)

Canopy layer
95 ft. (29 m)

Understory
55 ft. (17 m)

Undergrowth
15 ft. (5 m)

Human
Habitat   =   Abundant
Edible and useful
Diversity

Human Habitat

Zooming into a continental view of North America, we see a kaleidoscope of ecosystem habitats. The establishment of human habitat has always been driven by accessibility to edible ecosystems. We have traditionally migrated for this abundance and still orient our daily and yearly routines around food and depend on biodiversity for societal success.

What Is Habitat?

Habitat is the environment where an organism (bee, bear, or butterfly) lives. A habitat can be a hollow log or an entire forest, depending on the how far the organism has to travel to find its necessities. A bear's "bare necessities," as Baloo famously sang, would have consisted of food (honey, berries, insects), water, shelter, and community. The area that provides access to these necessities is what defines a bear's habitat.

Diverse Edible Ecosystem Abundance

Every creature has its home and is adapted to its unique climate and mixture of species. Human adaptation to diverse environments has occurred over millions of years. We now occupy every single terrestrial biome on Earth* and nestle into many of its more challenging ecosystems. But, in particular, we are **drawn to areas with diverse edible and useful abundance.** These are our habitats.

* Humans have only recently set up permanent habitat in Antarctica, but come on, you know what I mean!

We (yellow) are intrinsically linked to the environment (red) and made our habitat in diverse and abundant ecosystems with many companionship species (blue).

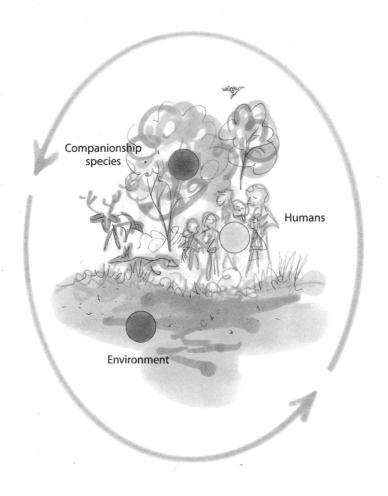

Companionship species

Humans

Environment

Human Habitat

Edible ecosystems, such as fruiting woodlands or berry meadows, make up our **ancestral human habitat**. *Homo sapiens* **evolved** within edible ecosystems, and our cultures and civilizations formed from this diverse ecological abundance. Ecosystems provided life-giving goods and services, generating wealth, technology, and community. Ecosystems also offered challenges such as disease, competition for food, and lack of shelter; still, we prospered and spread around the globe on the foundation of biodiversity.

Abundant Edge

All ecosystems have edges where they meet other ecosystems; at *ecotones*,* there is a gradual shift in species complexity across the landscape. This change can also be abrupt.

Living organisms interact with each other as a community. Ancestral communities relied on the interrelationship of the various parts of an ecosystem.

For instance, a cliff can divide an upland grass ecosystem from a seaside ecosystem below, such as we see along the cliffs of Dover, England.

Whether gradual or abrupt, the edges of ecosystems are very diverse. The principle of edge diversity is well documented. For instance, there is a marked abundance in riparian ecosystems (where land and water meet), as well as woodland ecosystems (where open grasslands meet dense forest). A famous example is the edges that occur within a tropical rainforest, where towering trees and multi-layered canopies create distinct vertical ecosystem strata above a single acre of land. Biodiversity flourishes amidst the many **ecological niches** created vertically and horizontally in a mature forest where different environmental conditions (sunlight, moisture, heat) and ecosystem dynamics occur. For instance, different species of birds are found at different canopy layers; in the emergent layer are found many birds of prey where they can spot their game, whereas in the canopy layer there may be more fruit-loving birds.

* A transitional area between two distinct ecosystems (field and forest) on a local scale, or biomes (boreal forest and prairie) on a regional scale.

Proximity to Edible Abundance

Humans have always been drawn to these **ecological edges**, especially those full of edible and useful abundance. We migrated between and settled areas of biodiversity. We were inspired by their bounty and gathered seasonally to enjoy it, to save it for later, and prepare for its return. Our wealth and health were entwined with edible ecological abundance. Edible ecosystems provided for our needs and proximity to them meant survival. For 200,000 years, human evolution was influenced by accessibility to ecosystem abundance. *Humans that could find, harness, and maximize an ecosystem's yields became leaders and progenitors.* It was the "survival of the food-finding fittest," and this means our bodies and minds are tuned to this ecosystem origin. It was—and will be—societies that regenerate this biodiversity that stand the test of time.

Mesolithic petroglyphs in Rajat Prapat, India, depict an abundant cliffside honey harvest from Apis dorsata.[2]

Ecosystem Evolution

Humans evolved within wild ecosystems. Our physical bodies, minds, and nervous systems adapted to the dynamic and diverse nature around us. We were surrounded by the sights, smells, sounds, and textures of ecosystems. They engaged our bodies, minds, and spirits.

The human body, mind, and nervous system haven't evolved much since we left the wild edible ecosystems. What has changed is our culture. Much of what makes the humans of today different from those of 10,000 years ago is what we are taught from a young age. Our differences are mostly learned and less genetic. If you took a human of 5,000 years ago and plunked them down in the middle of Manhattan, they would probably have a panic attack, but if you brought them up as a child, they could be taught to drive a car or negotiate a grocery store as well as the average person today.

We have the potential to reteach **ecosystem intimacy** and mentor stewardship at a young age. This could create generational change, leading to more ubiquitous ecosystem health and wealth.

"We love nature because we learned to love the things that helped us survive. We feel comfortable in nature because that is where we have lived for most of life on Earth. We are genetically determined to love the natural world. It is in our DNA."

— Dr. Qing Li[3]

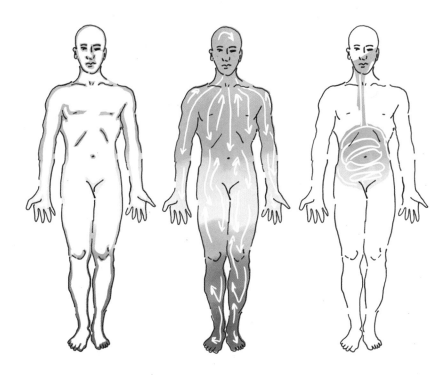

Our minds, bodies, and nervous system are hardwired for the wild, original nature we evolved within.

Ecosystem Within

There is an entire microcosm of life within, on, and around us. The human species evolved within ecosystems, and they evolved within us. Our intestines, stomach, and other organs are teeming with microorganisms that form a micro-ecosystem (**the microbiome**). We are habitat to some 100 trillion microbes.[4] There are significantly more "good bugs" than "bad bugs" in our bodies, and they improve our health in such ways *as aiding in the digestion of our food and improving our immune system*.

When we live in a healthy environment and eat nutritious food, breathe clean air, and drink good water, our microbiome is more likely to be in a state of homeostasis, and we remain healthy and optimally functional.[5] Our microbiome is full of life, and when we are exposed to toxins or neglect necessities, this upsets the balance of a healthy living system within us. Complexity requires complexity to maintain a balance. When our internal biodiversity is lost, we no longer can benefit from their many services.

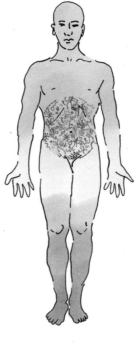

We are within our ecosystem, and the ecosystem is within us. Diversity provides many benefits, and balance comes from a healthy habitat inside and out.

Ecological Niche

An organism's ecological niche is its role within the ecosystem community. Its niche encompasses the resources and services it uses and those it provides. Humans have a broad niche; we are generalists, meaning we can make do in many situations. We have adapted to different climates, and we can eat almost anything—from oysters to arugula. As generalists, we have been able to migrate and settle almost the entire globe and have carried foods from the major centers of plant domestication with us. We are significant dispersers of food plants and seeds. This influence on the propagation of edible ecosystems is part of our ecological niche. *What is your ecological niche?* How do you contribute to your community? Let's reimagine this role as **food plant dispersers** in our modern context: What life forms exist within your community currently or might exist with a change in the landscape? And where do you currently receive ecosystem benefits, such as food, from? Is it possible to have these nearer to home, and could you be a catalyst for this change? The answer is yes, and it is a very human attribute for us all to influence the edible landscape of our communities.

Like humans, butterflies are found in almost all terrestrial ecosystems, and they also migrate long distances. Their niche includes eating the leaves of plants when they are caterpillars; then, as butterflies, they dine on the nectar and help the plants cross-pollinate.

Thrive or Survive

Are you thriving or surviving? If you give contributions to your community and receive resources and services in return, you exist within a balanced niche. Humans want to thrive and not just survive, but when we thrive within a global system, we need to provide global support for the regeneration of the ecosystems that support us. When an individual's contributions and returns are local and direct, a community is more sustainable and resilient. As Theodore Roosevelt said, "The nation behaves well if it treats its natural resources as assets which it must turn over to the next generation increased, and not impaired, in value."[6]

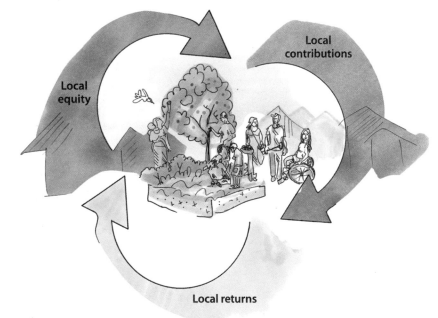

Local contributions

Local equity

Local returns

The Acceleration of Land Use

The human desire to thrive rather than just survive is what drove humans to change how we interacted with the land. We began to domesticate and cultivate diversity to secure our sources of wealth and well-being nearer to home and to manage seasonal productivity. This tendency to desire a better life is not a bad thing, but it did drive us down a road of intensive ecological intervention, and what seemed like a good idea—agriculture and technological development—is now on a crash course.

Humans' abilities to organize our ecosystems accelerated generation to generation, society to society. With the advent of modern technology and urbanization, the power of humans' ability to shape natural systems outstripped the pace at which natural systems could regenerate themselves. We are exceeding the biocapacity of our planet. This has consequences for human health and societal wealth if we run out of what we need to thrive and survive.

Montreal was built on an island of diverse abundance and could be returned to this biodiversity as part of a new cultural landscape.

Past

Present

Future

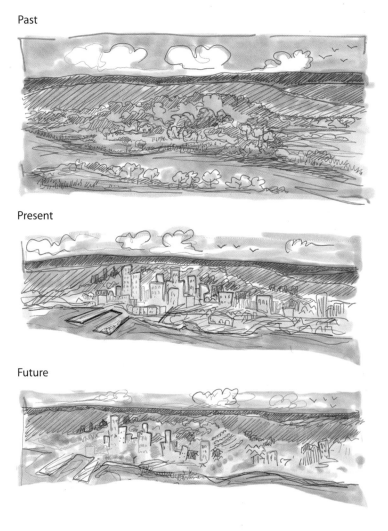

Short-Term Gains and Long-Term Pains

There are three pitfalls to the seemingly incredible achievements of human-kind and our development model:

1. **Our Societal Success Is Non-regenerative:** Despite our capacity to "conquer nature," ecosystems remain the source of our **societal wealth**, and unsustainable and non-regenerative practices will ultimately be our demise. The significance of ecosystem goods and services for human society can be seen across all of our cultural practices. Most human needs are met directly from our environment and biosphere.

2. **Our Health and Wellness Is Not a Priority:** Arguably our best preventative measure and remedy against disease is to live a healthy lifestyle in a clean environment. Human cognitive development moves faster than our physical evolution. Our bodies are accustomed to the qualities of a biodiverse world, and the monoculture model of land-use planning is undermining our primary health.

3. **Globalization Means Global Consequences:** We are no longer simply locally or regionally effecting change. Our non-regenerative socio-economic model is affecting the global life-support systems. In a way, we are *too* adept at survival for the *now*, rather than for long-term success. History shows that societies will *cut the last tree*, as they did on Easter Island. Communities with access to diversity thrived; those who didn't manage it sustainably expanded, warred, and collapsed.[7]

Our pattern of using up resources, overpopulating an area, and then expanding our catchment area is getting old. Today, the catchment area is already global. It cannot be further expanded without seriously jeopardizing the cornerstone of our wealth and wellness: biodiversity and life-supporting ecosystems. Caring for your backyard is responsible sustainability. If you are accessing wealth from a global resource pool, then your responsibility grows. Frankly, humans are not capable of tracking responsible purchases on such a global scale, and political and corporate "fair trade" and "green" actions are rarely regenerative and equitable. It is better for communities to maximize the production of needed foods, and other ecosystem goods and services near-to-home and then import and export responsibly with other communities.

If there were ever a time to move on to the next stage in human land management, it is now. Edible ecosystem land planning provides for essential needs through community models, such as local farmers markets, community gardens, backyard orchards, pick-your-own hedgerows, and edible bike lanes.

Human innovation has and will continue to forge new ways forward using our cognitive might. Mightier still would be reimagining our place within natural systems and focusing our ingenuity on ecosystem solutions that will meet current and future needs.

Most modern communities have built up an ecological deficit because the population's ecological footprint exceeds their regional biocapacity. Community use of resources and need for ecosystem services is far beyond the local ecosystem's capacity to renew them. Thus, our demand for goods and services is being met by far-off ecological reserves in areas where biocapacity is higher, and the local footprint is lower. But, globally, this is reaching a critical threshold of global footprint surpassing global biocapacity.[12]

Biocapacity and Ecological Footprint

An **ecological footprint** is a measure of our impact on Earth's life-support systems (demand and supply of Earth's ecological assets). These goods and services include the production of food, timber, and water, as well as the filtration and absorption of our regular and toxic waste. **Biocapacity** for any community, city, or region is a measure of ecological productivity, including the hectares needed for grazing, forest, and cropland, as well as fisheries and spaces for housing and infrastructure.

We would need five Earths to support society if everyone today had the same ecological footprint of the average North American.[8] Vancouver is considered an eco-conscious city, but even there, the ecological footprint is huge. Vancouver's total ecological footprint in 2006 was 10,071,670 gha (global hectares)*; this is about 36 times larger than the metro area itself.[9] Food production has the most significant impact on Vancouver's ecological footprint (which includes accounting for the land needed to produce food and the carbon sequestration required to offset the production and transport emissions).[10]

Another study found that the average UK resident had a carbon footprint** of 12.12 tonnes of CO_2. (This is the amount of emissions resulting from one person's use of ecosystem goods and services, direct and indirect).[11] As human populations continue to grow, and in consideration of a growing middle class globally, we will find our ecological footprint is reaching the Earth's biocapacity—its ability to sustain us with resources and services such as air, water, and food.

* The global hectare abbreviated as (gha) is the measurement unit for ecological footprint and biocapacity accounting. According to the Global Footprint Network, it is "a globally comparable and standardized hectare with world average productivity."

** Carbon footprint is the measure of total emissions caused by an individual, company, or nation. It is a factor in our ecological footprint and is currently a major cause of anthropogenic climate change.

Natural Capital Loss

We are losing our natural capital—the wealth that is responsible for all of human success and is still our primary source of societal wealth and well-being. Topsoil, old-growth forest, clean air, and water—all our ecosystems are being consumed, polluted, and degraded. Top on the list of concerns is the loss of biodiversity. We are in the midst of the **sixth major extinction Earth** has experienced during its 4.3 billion years of formation and evolution. The importance of this loss of wealth is incalculable. The preservation of biodiversity could yield pharmaceutical discoveries, new foods, and remediation of toxins in our soil and water. The simple economic value of our natural wealth is immense, and there is so much biodiversity we haven't begun to benefit from in our current development model. We need to evaluate diverse wild ecosystems before we replace them with low-diversity land use, while also redesigning our typical development to be more diversified. An approach to land use planning that focuses on diversity will regenerate our natural capital and strengthen our societal resilience.

On traditional grazing land in Mongolia, a gully is opening up as a result of compaction from motorbike and truck traffic that ranges across the grasslands. My guide told me these areas were flat just ten years earlier, but little changes in the land from tire ruts led to the flooding and erosion that has now produced extensive gullies. Our ecological footprint can be improved through good design and care for landscapes.

Learning about pollinator species, from bees to butterflies, their benefits, and habitats is a great outdoor activity. Humans have been enjoying city parks and the great outdoors for centuries, and now we can build upon this with an enthusiasm for the ecosystem services the spaces provide, creating new pollinator gardens, and reducing harmful toxins.

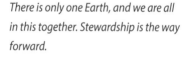

Stewards

Now, for the first time in history, an individual's ecological niche is global. We cannot really manage being a responsible consumer and meaningful contributor on this scale. Clearly, humans have a high capacity to alter ecosystems—primarily for short-term gain. For humans to truly thrive on planet Earth, we need to embrace our ecological niche as *stewards of the ecosystem, not exploiters*. Some of the principles about how to do this can be found in humanity's past, though we will need to reinvent and reinterpret them in light of humanity's present.

Stewardship

Stewardship is the responsible planning and management of our resources. It can be applied to various professions, a property, or the environment as a whole. Our society's stewardship of Earth's natural capital might include both a community's stewardship of single forest or an individual's stewardship of their yard. Stewardship is a critical part of societal success—through stewardship, we protect ecosystems so they can function for our benefit. It is also something that needs to be incorporated into every business, taught to our children at a young age, and recognized as one of the most important new "green" job opportunities of the future.

There is only one Earth, and we are all in this together. Stewardship is the way forward.

We can go somewhere we have never been before. Our true niche lies within **accessible biodiversity**, which, by definition, mandates the regeneration and growth of our habitats. We should all participate in this and enjoy the results. With the right design framework for landscape transition and generational changes bringing new ethics and aesthetics, localizing many ecosystem goods and services can become the norm for our global society.

Stewardship is a powerful means of making change through exemplifying, mentoring, and sponsoring change in our communities (this will be discussed further in Section 5).

Ancestral Ecosystems

Coming close into the Northeastern United States and Eastern Canada, we find areas of diverse, edible, and useful abundance. The ecosystems of this area consisted of fertile floodplains, upland woodlands, rich grasslands, and abundant estuaries, streams, and many small and great lakes. These ancestral ecosystems upheld human health and wealth.

Traditional Land Use

Traditionally, wild and diverse abundances attracted communities of the genus *Homo* to live within edible ecosystems (200,000 to ~30,000 BP*). We migrated and spread across the globe, adapting to a variety of ecosystems and environments. Eventually, humans began to nurture edible diversity for improved habitat (~30,000 to 10,000 BP), and finally, we began to domesticate wild plants and animals and modify our habitat to become farms and communities (the last 10,000 BP). Let's look at some examples of ancestral edible ecosystems and traditional land use.

* A measure of years Before Present ("present" is often given as 1950).

Humans migrated with seasonal abundance and made use of different edible ecosystems, such as visits to seaside richness and upland fruit forests.

A Place Named "Abundance"

The Puye Cliff Dwellings in northern New Mexico were populated between 900 to 1580 A.D. by 1,500 Tewa people, the ancestors of the Khap'oe Ówîngeh community (Santa Clara Pueblo). This abundant human habitat is found at the base and the top of Parajito Plateau, a mesa nestled against the Jemez Mountains with its towering Tsikumu P'in (Jemez Peak). It looks across the Rio Grande Basin to the Sangre de Cristo Mountains in the east with the lofty K'use P'in (Truchas Peak). Between these great mountain ranges lie diverse ecosystems that provided many natural and cultural resources for the surrounding traditional communities. The Rio Grande and Pojoaque rivers flow nearby, and the Santa Clara Creek is within a short walk of the caves and Pueblo dwellings of Puye. Here, cliffs offered shelter from winter storms, while in summer, the Tewa lived in houses on top of the mesa. Summer rains and snowmelt from the surrounding mountains and mesa fed gardens of corn, beans, and squash in the fertile valley below.

This was a land of abundance.

This was also the habitat for many useful species of medicinal plants, animals, and edible mushrooms. Indeed, the word "Puye" means "Where the Rabbits Gather or Mate," alluding to the local abundance of rabbits as a result of the ecotone between pinyon-juniper woodlands, savannah and mixed-conifer forests. Place naming based on natural occurrences of bio-diversity was common globally, including the great metropolis of Chicago,

"Puye" means "Where the Rabbits Gather" in the Tewa language. Many indigenous place names refer directly to the diversity of an area. Now, place names like "Ridgewood" and "Prairie Point" make little sense amidst their utter lack of woodland or prairie abundance.

whose name is derived from a Myaamia (Miami) word for wild garlic, which grew profusely in that area. Rabbit was an important food source for these people and remains one today for many around the world.

"We go rabbit hunting often," says Talavi, who grew up in the neighboring Ohkay Ówîngeh community and is passionate about Traditional Ecological Knowledge (TEK). "We use rabbits for both cultural and natural resources." She explained that the first pair of moccasins for newborn babies are made of rabbit fur and that a rite of passage for young boys is hunting rabbits. The Tewa culture is steeped in an appreciation of biodiversity and a holistic use of its resources. "However," says Talavi, "much of this culture is being lost due to colonialism, and traditional knowledge is not being passed down to younger generations."

Lowland and upland forests provided pinyon nuts, juniper berries, ponderosa pine poles, and much more. There were many useful animals, including squirrels, elk, bison, deer, and many birds. "Many people used to go to Santa Clara canyon near Puye area to collect mushrooms in a good wet year," says Talavi, who has a Master's in Conservation Biology and Environmental Science (TCBES) and is currently working at Flowering Tree Permaculture, "and there are many medicinal plants that grow abundantly, like juniper, sage, cholla cactus, four-wing saltbush, and greasewood." Talavi and other Tewa descendants are concerned with the destruction of the land, the loss of biodiversity, and the loss of traditional knowledge under a modern paradigm.

A pictograph showing a traditional harvest of multi-colored Hopi corn.[13] Seed-saving events in New Mexico and elsewhere are helping spread Hopi blue corn and other essential staples for food security and cultural heritage. Note: Corn grown by Ibrahim Loeks.

*The Hopi culture has saved heirloom corn, beans, and squash for thousands of years. A return to local seed saving and the selection of **site-suitable varieties** is a big part of the food security solution for our modern society.*

Tien Shan Fruit Forests

In the Tien Shan Mountains, ranging across 2000 miles in Kazakhstan, Uzbekistan, and Turkmenistan lie the last remnants of a forest that has been evolving for millions of years.[14] It is a wild fruit forest full of diverse edible and useful plant species, including many in the famous Rosacea family. One of these plants is the famed fruit from the garden of Eden, that round red beauty that allegedly knocked sense into Sir Isaac Newton's head and now graces many cellphones and computers as a symbol of good design. Yes, the infamous apple!

The ancestor of all modern apples is *Malus sieversii*, an ancient species that still grows in the mountains around the former Kazakhstan capital city of Almaty, a place name meaning "the Father of Apples." It is here that a botanical garden has been set up by Aimak Dzangaliev as part of an effort to preserve these ancient groves. Aimak Dzangaliev, (a guy who could be likened to a fusion of Johnny Apple Seed and Indiana Jones) spent a lifetime searching through remote central Asian mountains, finding, documenting, and conserving rare wild apple trees and their genetics against a backdrop of deforestation and development.

Research and exploration over the last few centuries have revealed that the valleys, floodplains, and hillsides of this region are the birthplaces of the apple and other significant plants. Apples are the third most-produced fruit today, with 83 million metric tons produced in 2017.[15] The poppy, also "born" in this part of the world, has been a medicinal plant to humans for thousands of years and is a traditional seasoning for food preparation.

A Diverse and Wild Ecosystem

Malus sieversii still grows as part of a diverse and layered ecology. And growing alongside a myriad of wild apple varieties can be found raspberries, blackberries, currants, roses, hawthorns, tulips, peonies, apricots, almonds, pears, rhubarb, hops, poplars, spruce, and a plethora of edible and medicinal herbs, including the humble garlic and the revered poppy.

The diversity of the Tien Shan fruit forests is staggering, and their significance for food security today comes from their genetic potential to help us breed new varieties that are more drought-tolerant, pest-resistant, and cold hardy, as well as other important traits.

Domestication

One of the significant ways we tended the wild was through the selection of food plant seeds that suited us better. Initially, this was accidental. For instance, humans in ancient Mesopotamia brought about a shift to more *sessile* wheat grains (meaning they stayed on the plant and made harvest easier). How did this come about? The easiest grains to harvest were the ones with the genetic trait of sessile seeds. These seeds were brought back to human communities. In the compost heaps of the villages and along the trails they traveled, early humans incidentally spread the seeds from plants that included the trait of having sessile seeds. Accidental selection was part of the **advent of domestication**, and, eventually, it led to the purposeful breeding of plants and animals based on human values.

Black emmer wheat is an heirloom food plant of significance. Humans have been growing and diversifying wheat for over 7,000 years. Wheat is currently one of the most planted crops in the world. Ancient grains have significantly higher levels of beneficial fiber and minerals than modern varieties—and less gluten and a lower glycemic index, to boot.[16]

Apple Selection and Diversity

Let's consider the time timeline of apple domestication to show the great efforts we have made to create the heirloom food plants we have today. Humans have been a powerful force behind both the diversification and loss of food varieties.

1. **The wild apple**, *Malus sieversii*, originated in the Tien Shan Mountains.

2. Early humans applied **selective pressure inadvertently** by choosing some wild apples over others to eat.

3. Apple trees with the genetic variability of **our initial selective pressure** went feral around our communities. As these midden groves matured, they would have undergone further selection; again and again, humans chose the apples they liked best, ate them, and tossed away those cores that contained the seeds that would produce more trees.

4. Then, humans made a switch from this inadvertent selection **to purposeful domestication**. We began to plant orchards; we became sedentary and passed on the knowledge of selective breeding. The first successful varieties are known as "landraces."

5. Apples spread globally, and more breeding yields **locally adapted heirloom cultivars**.

6. **Now, only a handful of varieties** appear on grocery store shelves, but new breeding is always needed.

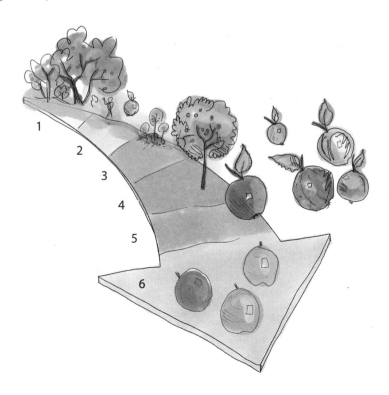

Squash, ready to be transplanted with seeds of companion plants: heirloom pole beans, blue corn, sunflowers, and nasturtiums.

Food Plant Guild

The companionship planting of corn, beans, and squash—otherwise known as the *three sisters*—was cultivated in mounds by Pueblo and other indigenous communities across North America. Corn provides a trellis for the beans to climb; beans fix nitrogen in association with nitrogen-fixing bacteria in the soil, and squash is the perfect groundcover to conserve moisture and prevent weed growth. This companionship of food plants for mutual benefit and improved production for humans is called a *guild*.

Wild Plant Guilds

Plants in the wild often grow as guilds, and this was undoubtedly the inspiration for traditional farmers during the advent of agriculture. In the Southwest, you can find plants growing together in spots of no more than five feet by five feet. They form very clear companionships, helping conserve moisture through a microclimate effect, improving the soil for each other, cooling each other's roots, and hosting diverse life forms to enhance pollination and seed dispersal. Although they compete somewhat for limited resources of sunlight, water, and space, they mostly partition these resources through different shapes, depth, and heights of their roots, trunks, and branches. They also access the resources they require at different times of the year and day.

A wild grouping of pinyon pine (Pinus edulis), yucca (Yucca baccata), and prickly pear cactus (Opuntia lindheimeri) share resources and support each other in a companionship guild.

Pinyon pine

Yucca

Prickly pear cactus

We Began with Polyculture

Polyculture, or the production of diverse plants together as a guild, has played an important role in traditional agriculture. The earliest forms of human agriculture were immersed within ecosystems. Then we mimicked their diversity, form, and function in our cultural landscapes. The geographic points of food plant domestication and origin were also epicenters of diversified farming practices. Eventually, we increasingly segregated food plants into monoculture plots as people moved to cities and agriculture was industrialized. This is making our society vulnerable. When you put all your eggs in one basket, you may crack them all if you trip and fall. Pests and disease spread through monocultures like wildfire, and societies dependent on fewer plant species are less resilient if this happens. Diverse food systems are less prone to pests and more resilient when disease occurs.

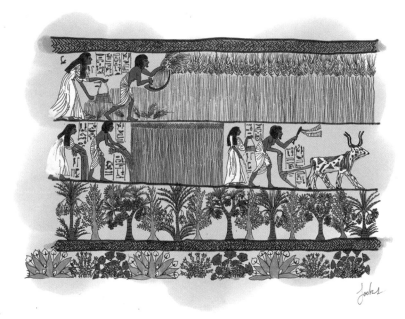

Egyptians grew wheat and barley and intercropped trees, shrubs, and herbs, as evidenced from petroglyph farming scenes on the walls of ancient buildings.[17] Their success was based on nutrient-laden flood water and diverse food plants; their failure was limiting access to this wealth to only a select few people.

These wild and domesticated plants have been grown and eaten in the mountain communities of Guerrero, Mexico for generations as part of a biodiverse land management system that dates back to the original inhabitants of Mesoamerica.

Chinese Polyculture

Another place of food plant origin is southeastern China. Here, the land has been in continuous farming for millennia.[18] This is the place of origin for many of the fruits, animals, and grains that are valued around the world. The fact that this area has been continuously and intensively farmed for so long provides a window into the success of **diversity as a land-use planning strategy**.

The ancient Chinese food system integrated rice paddies with fish, ducks, and fruit trees. The rice was planted into terraced paddies that filled with water; fish lived in these waters fertilizing the rice and eating pests. Ducks were moved through the paddies after the rice was harvested to clear out any additional pests. Along the edges of the paddies, medicinal and edible herbs, berries, and fruit were grown. Modern aquaponics demonstrates some of these early polycultural principles.

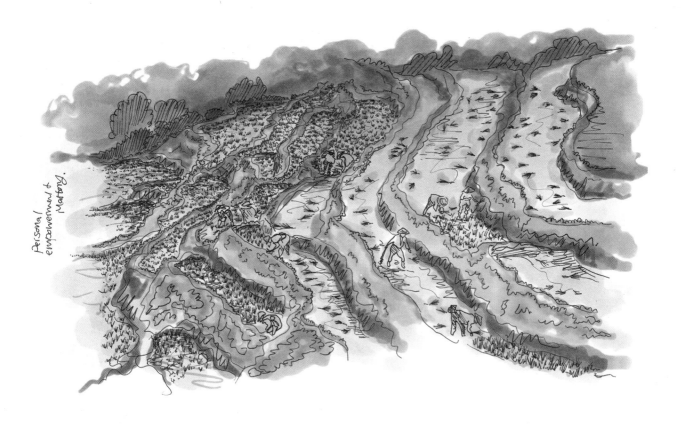

The Cultural Revolution in China resulted in a significant loss of diversity and fostered starvation when it consolidated and industrialized farming. China is now at the forefront of reforestation, and diversified small-plot agriculture is again on the rise.

Remnant Ecosystem Abundance

Abundances like those in ancient Egypt and pre-Revolutionary China can still be found in our society today. Ecosystems can proffer up many fruits, berries, nuts, herbs, and edible and medicinal mushrooms, as well as diverse animals and other products, like applewood for the barbeque. The boreal forests in Northern Quebec are full of edible mushrooms and wild blueberries. Yet, these wild abundances are not only in the far-off wilds. A quiet park outside Winnipeg, Manitoba, offers visitors raspberries, chokecherries, saskatoons, hazelnuts, cranberries, and other delicacies. This area used to be a quarry and a homestead and was set aside as a park in 1965, but before that, it was a prairie and aspen woodland ecosystem.[19]

Chanterelles picked in a forest and hazelnuts found along an old farm hedgerow in an expanding suburb are examples of yields from remnant ecosystems.

Twenty-five pounds of chokecherries can be harvested in a few hours of an enjoyable walkabout.

Endangered Edible Ecosystems

One of the most endangered edible ecosystems on the planet is the tallgrass prairie. There is less than 1% of this ecosystem remaining. The ecological edge between tallgrass prairie, aspen parkland, and upland oak forests was a vibrant environment for human societal success. The Dakota and Ojibway communities of present-day Manitoba built their communities on the biodiversity of this region. The grasslands were lush with edible, medicinal, and useful herbs. Berry-rich shrublands provided seasonally nutrient-dense chokecherries, saskatoons, pin cherries, raspberries, and gooseberries. Upland woodlands proffered rose, hawthorn, acorns, and woodland herbs.

Chokecherries and hawthorn are nutrient-dense fruits that can still be powerful food sources in our diets today, whether fresh, in jams, or teas. Wild foods have nutrition often lacking in more over-the-counter fruits that have less nutrient-density as a consequence of farming practices and variety breeding.

On an island in Algonquin Park, with shallow soil and buffeted by winds, a woodland ecosystem was still able to yield bountifully. Here, I was able to dine on wild berries with the lushness, freshness, and sensations of the ecosystem around me. It seems strange to have to drive to a provincial park and canoe out to an island to find a space so nurturing.

Edible Ecosystem Significance

Diverse and edible landscapes were very significant for early humans. The significance of these ecosystems is revealed in archeological digs, as petroglyphs and pictographs, and in historical records. Plants have played an essential role in our cultural innovations. For instance, some of the earliest records of human writing consist of cuneiform* records of grain harvest in Sumeria. The following pages will illustrate society's origin in ecosystem abundance and the historical record of this throughout many aspects of society.

* Ancient writing on clay tablets.

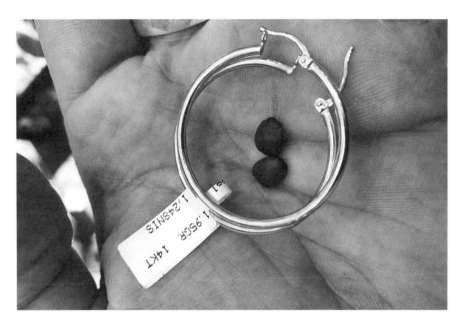

Carob seeds, now enjoyed as a chocolate alternative, were also used as a tool by serving as counterweights in markets for measuring the relative value of precious goods, such as gold. Vestiges of this historical use can be found in the word karat, used to denote the purity of gold and diamonds. Everywhere we walk, we find evidence of the importance of food plants to human culture, even in the paving stones of our edifices.

This olive grove gave shade to those listening to the words of Jesus in the garden of Gethsemane.

Cornucopia, a symbol of abundant diversity, is an ancient image. This coat-of-arms shows the significance of natural wealth and accessibility as the key to success. But underneath, above, and around any cornucopia is the source of its abundance: the environment and ecology, which require stewardship if they are to be sustained.

In Mesoamerica, cacao was a revered and sacred plant used to make a traditional drink. It was also a currency for the Mayan civilization; the cacao beans, from which we make chocolate, were a means of barter, tribute, and exchange. Today, chocolate is a multi-billion-dollar industry. Yet the diversity of cacao trees is being lost to monoculture plantations.

Back and to the Future

This book is not advocating that we live in the past. Let's be on board to live in a future we haven't yet seen—one that values where we have been as a human species within Earth's ecosystems and where we are as modern societies with abundant ecosystem needs. Let's find the next step. We long existed in nature. Being regenerative is simply the practical thing to do for our society, economy, and the environment.

Solutions and Opportunities

OURS IS A WORLD DIVIDED, where we live is not where our food comes from. Only in the last few hundred years have we seen the complete segregation of human communities from human resources. What was once an integrated human habitat is now an urban/rural divide. What was once edible ecosystem is now a monoculture resource landscape, and the produce gets trucked to centralized stores for shoppers to select weeks-old foods. This is part of the cause of many issues that face us today, from poverty and food insecurity to cancer, depression, and obesity. Yet, our modern social, economic, and environmental dilemmas have solutions: a redesign of our landscape. Actually, the contemporary world has many opportunities for transitioning landscapes and transforming the way we live and eat. We must see and seize these opportunities and build better community.

Habitat Lost

Now we zoom into the region around the island of Montreal in Quebec—situated where the Saint Lawrence and Ottawa meet, and near Lake Champlain and the Laurentian Mountains. Its potential includes fertile growing lands, lush forests, and riparian abundance. This **abundant edge** attracted humans to this area 8,000 years ago because it was a crossroads of ecological diversity. Our relationship to this landscape is changing, but its potential remains in many places, and new opportunities exist.

What Is Our Cultural Landscape?

The **cultural landscape** is the human-made landscape: neighborhoods, industrial complexes, farmlands, planted forests, and city parks. It is the landscape where we live, work, and play. It is a powerful concept because it is a product of how *we manage our environs*, and this is where we spent *most of our time*. Living in our modern society begs the question: how do we want to live? Moving through fruit-lined neighborhoods or a concrete jungle are both possibilities—we choose what we make of our communities. Yes, cultural landscapes are a product of the regional environment and land management history, but they are also shaped by a continuum of cultural values and decision-making. We have the potential to shape our cultural landscape every day through how we develop new land and redevelop existing land use!

Decision-making that determines how land is developed—into roads, farming, and neighborhoods, for example—should be informed by what humans need on a local, regional, and global scale. What ecosystem services can new development provide? How sustainable is this development? As this book will show, **prioritizing biodiverse greenspaces** improves our communities and provides for a prosperous and healthy society into the future.

We need to reenvision a multifunctional landscape architecture and build true habitat for humanity.

Human Habitat Relationship

Human habitat relationships have followed a trajectory over thousands of years. At first, we lived within **wild ecosystems** that provided for us, and we evolved fitness, adapting to our biodiverse surroundings and nurturing their suitability to our societal well-being. Then we began developing a **cultural landscape**, with settlements, agriculture, and an increasing diversity of edible and useful species. When we had access to wild and domestic abundance, we thrived. Eventually, we entered a phase of **habitat loss**. This included drastic declines in biodiversity, the separation of production under monoculture practices, and the segregation of human habitation from natural systems. We began to focus on the forest for its trees. Ecological landscapes became less a habitat and more about economies of industrial extraction and pollution. Accessibility to biodiversity stills governed wealth and health, but, increasingly, we have pushed people out of their habitat and built habitats that do not provide for life's necessities.

> "We abuse land because we regard it as a commodity belonging to us. When we see land as a community to which we belong, we may begin to use it with love and respect."
>
> — Aldo Leopold[1]

Traditional-Modern Land-Use Planning

One way to a healthy future is an approach to land-use planning and management that could be termed **traditional-modern.** In a traditional-modern approach, we need to recognize our 200,000 years of evolution in wild landscapes, while still honoring our current reality, taking the best of both for a positive future. We need to see the forest for more than just the trees and our yards for more than just grass.

> "We exist in a bizarre combination of Stone Age emotions, medieval beliefs, and god-like technology."
>
> — E.O. Wilson[2]

Modern Situation

There have been some marked changes in the ecosystem due to the development of agriculture, urbanization, and the suburban dream: 1) biodiversity loss, 2) monoculture land planning and management, and 3) segregation of human habitation from natural and cultural ecosystems.

We hold the future in our hands—our landscape is our future, and where we all stand, at this moment, is where we can make a stand, make a mark, pick up a shovel and plant our future.

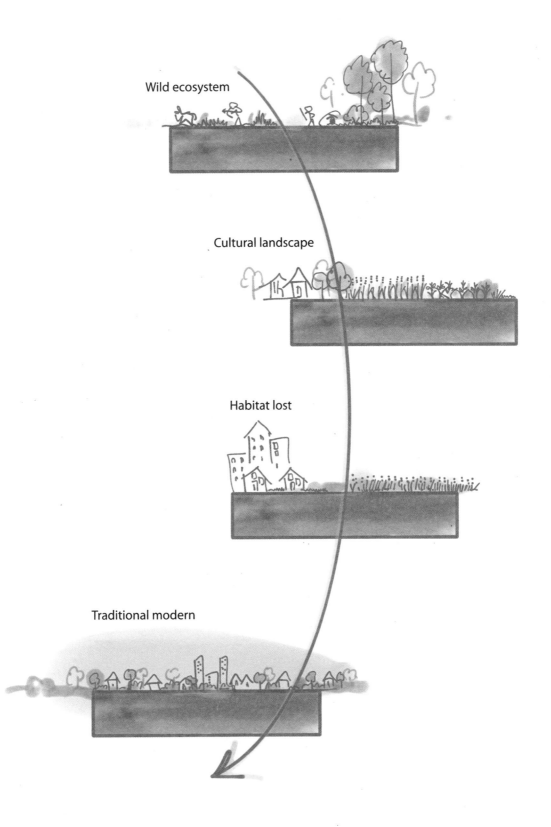

Biodiversity Loss

There has been an increasingly drastic decline in biodiversity over the last 300 years. Although our planet has faced mass extinction before, the current rate of extinction is due to human land use. Species are being lost primarily due to habitat destruction, fragmentation, and pollution. Research shows the heterogeneity of land is important for sustaining biodiversity.[3] For farms, this can include regenerative farming practices and maintenance of wild lands, hedgerows, and bush lots. In more urban areas, this includes prioritizing greenbelts, diverse parklands, riparian buffers, and wild spaces. We need a mosaic of varied land use to maintain diversity. Biodiversity supports ecosystems and ecosystems support biodiversity; both support the life systems of our planet on which we depend. Our society is dependent on three forms of diversity: genetic, species, and ecosystem. All are being lost—drained away.

"The worst thing that will probably happen—in fact is already well underway—is not energy depletion, economic collapse, conventional war, or the expansion of totalitarian governments. As terrible as these catastrophes would be for us, they can be repaired in a few generations. The one process now going on that will take millions of years to correct is loss of genetic and species diversity by the destruction of natural habitats. This is the folly our descendants are least likely to forgive us."

— E.O. Wilson[4]

Endangered and Extinct Species

This biodiversity loss is quite drastic and is putting in jeopardy many species throughout Earth's biomes. According to the IUCN (International Union for Conservation of Nature) Red List of Threatened Species, more than 28,000 species are currently threatened with extinction (from an assessment of just 105,700 species). The rates of the current mass extinction are far above pre-human extinction rates, indicating that we are entering Earth's sixth major extinction.[5] This time, human impact is a major cause. The past five extinctions were linked to cataclysmic events, such as extreme volcanic activity, sea-level rise, and meteor impact. Overall, these events caused disruption of food chains and inhospitable conditions for those species that died out. Today, the extinction event we are experiencing is **anthropogenic**—caused by pollution, habitat loss from development, and non-regenerative land management.

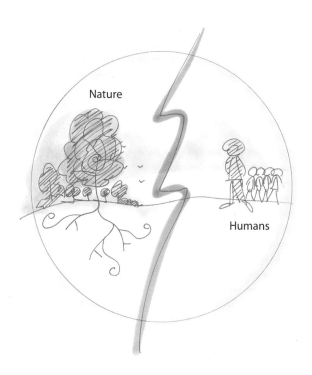

Ecosystem Diversity

The last remaining old-growth tropical rainforests are still being cut down for cropland, cattle, and development—even though these soils cannot sustain the production of crops without extensive inputs. Rainforest productivity in hot, humid climates and infertile soils depends on the quick cycling of nutrients using diverse ecosystem functions. The biodiversity of a single acre of tropical rainforest contains 20–86 tree species and hundreds of plants, animals, and other lifeforms. Although only 7% of Earth's land surface is covered by tropical rainforests, they contain half of the world's living species biodiversity[6] and have been continuously evolving for around 60 million years. Compared to the single crop of soy or corn it is being replaced with, we are looking at a *massive loss of ecosystem services for humanity.* It was estimated that 80,000 acres of tropical rainforest were lost daily in the early 2000s, and, despite notions that deforestation is waning, recent years have been considered the worst on record, with 39 million acres lost in 2017.[7] According to Global Forest Watch, the Brazilian Amazon lost an area of **primary forest** the size of Belgium in 2018; this old-growth forest is the most biologically diverse and the most threatened.[8]

We live a false dichotomy. Humans are not outside of nature. We are part of the natural system. It is easy to understand how we forget this: we are surrounded by high rises and responding to apps while hopping taxis across town or living in rural areas where 200-horsepower tractors harvest thousands of acres of soybeans a day. Nevertheless, we are still in the natural system, and when we remember this, it can help us work with the natural principles that govern our lives, our society's success, and our individual well-being.

Lost and Wasted

From the Arctic to the Amazon, our **primary ecosystems** are being destroyed and degraded for lumber, minerals, fossil fuels, and agriculture. We are failing to sufficiently address this loss of important genetic, species, and ecosystem diversity. Although these resources are important for society, an ecosystem approach to development could maximize the gain from any landscape without long-term harm to its other services. For now, let's look at how we can reduce the impact of food production on biodiversity.

Climate change is rapidly impacting the health of Arctic ecosystems and the communities that depend on them. According to Piita Irniq, a cultural teacher and spokesperson, "Inuit are inseparable from the land, and this is why we are concerned with its destruction." Land-use management is ready for a new paradigm, one in which people are more intimately connected with where their resources come from. A near-to-home management paradigm for many ecosystem goods and services makes landscape abuse more visible to modern society and helps shift how we relate to our cultural landscape.

Agrobiodiversity Loss

There is another kind of diversity being lost at a staggering rate: **agrobio-diversity**, or the diversity of our food plants. Agrobiodiversity is being jeopardized by global agribusiness, which is prioritizing the breeding of a select few varieties. Under the pressure of mechanized farming, global transport, and big-box grocery stores, we have less variety on our plates, the food is less nutritious, and the genetic variability within the food plants is severely reduced. Food plants have been selected to fit into a narrow range of valuable characteristics for a modern market. Namely, do they ripen together to facilitate mechanized harvest? Do they transport well (firmness)? Do they look good on a shelf? Important genetic characteristics that haven't been part of the equation over the last 50 years include nutritional value, cultural heritage, and genetic diversity.

The diversity of foodplants is staggering; even though we have lost so much, there is so much to enjoy and conserve.

Our Food Heritage

The food plants being lost are heirloom varieties that humans themselves created through selection over thousands of years. According to the FAO, we have lost 75% of food plant genetic diversity, and 75% of our food is now generated from only 5 animal and 12 plant species.[9] This loss has repercussions for farm sustainability and food security. We need diversity to design regenerative agriculture and allow us to breed more new varieties to meet new agri-dilemmas. Diversity is what allows agriculture to adapt to changing socio-economic and environmental circumstances.

The apple is being lost right in the backyard of Johnny Appleseed. Around 86% of apples that used to be grown in the United States are gone. Out of the 17,000 cultivars that used to be used for fresh eating, pie, juice, cider, and preserves, there are only 4,000 still grown in the US. What is more, 90% of apple production is composed of just 15 varieties.[10] We are losing the diversity we made alongside the greater biodiversity that has always sustained us.

Heirloom squashes and Guatemalan chilies.

We still have time to conserve biodiversity and increase our benefit from this abundant life.

Suburban Biodiversity

In suburban areas, the culprit for diversity loss is primarily strip-and-develop land planning, and it is perpetuated by the aesthetic of *lawn*, which is confounding, because, at our roots, we as humans are drawn to *biodiverse landscapes*. Although land planning of suburban communities could integrate more diversity from the get-go, most people choose to keep the land surrounding their houses in lawn and a few ornamentals. This concept of lawn is counterintuitive. Many humans actually have quite a wild aesthetic. How else to explain the weekend rush out of cities and suburbs to spend time in nature?

In urban areas, many are in search of habitat—wild, diverse spaces. We weekend away to the cottage, countryside, and forests; we are drawn to parks on sunny days and fill our homes with house plants and potted herbs on our balconies. We are in search of our habitat—the dynamic nature that provides us with well-being. "Weekends away" are cultural mechanisms to "bring us back" to our natural habitat.

Cities Grew on Diversity

Urban areas were once some of the most diverse and useful regions. One of the main reasons people originally settled in areas of the now-megacities, like New York, San Paolo, and Tokyo, is because there was good soil, accessible waters, and abundant diversity. Let's look at the region around Montreal, Canada, with a population of just over 4 million people. It is a similar size to about 100 cities globally, so it's a good representation of an average city.[11] This island was the meeting point of the Ottawa and Saint Lawrence rivers, which join to become the Saint Lawrence Seaway. This provided access to inland, riparian, and ocean biodiversity. It was also proximate to lush forests in the Laurentian Mountains to the North and the open, tillable lands of the Saint Lawrence Lowlands to the east, and the rich edge habitat of the stand-alone hills rising up from the flat plains of the Montérégie region. All in all, the island of Montreal was a crossroads of biodiversity. The urbanization of Montreal, as elsewhere, is the story of slowly paving, fragmenting, and degrading what made the area so desirable in the first place.

Montreal circa the 1500s to the 1700s tells a story of changes in the land, sociopolitical struggles for resources, and loss of regional biocapacity. The constant was its desirability to humans over the last 8,000 years because it had high biodiversity and biocapacity.

In the 1700s Montreal was increasingly deforested and the ecosystems altered, driven by the very desire of the landscape's ecological wealth.

Most of the land base of the island of Montreal is now developed. The primarily impermeable surfaces of pavement and the loss of forest and riparian areas are becoming major problems as climate change shifts the magnitude and frequency of flood events. The greenspaces in the city that are left are (ironically) thanks to their being former quarries, landfills, military parade ground, and cemeteries. Mount Royal itself was conserved, but sprawl has climbed its slopes.

Urban Biodiversity

Today, urban areas have minimal biodiversity because so much has been lost, but there is also much less greenspace available, and land-use planning focuses on a narrow range of landscape plants. Consider the urban canopy of a city like Winnipeg (another historical meeting point of biodiverse ecosystems). Currently, 60% of Winnipeg's urban forest is either elm or ash trees, and they are threatened by emerald ash borer and Dutch elm disease.[12]

Winnipeg has the most extensive remaining urban elm canopy in North America, with about 225,000 trees in its yards and along its rivers, streets, boulevards.[13] Now with Dutch elm disease, an introduced fungus that kills the tree, the city is threatened by an almost complete canopy loss and is paying millions to treat the trees each year. Although we can remedy this disease with treatments, they are ultimately just band-aid solutions. We need to organize to replant the urban forest—this time, having learned from our mistakes and making it a diverse forest.

Dutch elm disease causes the slow death of these popular street trees and has spread throughout central and eastern Canada, as well as the United States. In 2019, Winnipeg launched the One Million Tree Challenge to help reforestation efforts. Next, let's see this become the One Million Edible Ecosystem Spots Challenge! Homeowners, businesses, and institutions (alongside policymakers) can be putting energy and money into making our communities more biodiverse and sustainable.

Diversifying the City

Yes, we can plant a variety of city street trees. But we can also plant more fruit trees and an understory of plants, such as shrubs, bushes, flowers, and groundcovers. Approaching reforestation with an eye to diversity can actually reduce the cost of planting and long-term maintenance. For instance, the average cost of a tree planted in the city is about $800, yet many smaller, bare-root trees cost only $1 to $50. These trees are cheaper to plant, and, with proper planning and their increased vigor, they can soon surpass typical large trees in height and yield.

Companion planting should be used in municipal plantings. Bare-root saplings and whips* can thrive in the shelter of raspberries, hazelnuts, and currants as a nurse crop. The same goes for native species like big bluestem, saskatoons, and chokecherries. In Winnipeg, such an edible hedge could be nursed under the dead and dying elms trees, which themselves can be chipped down to mulch the new, young forest.

* Unbranched, young saplings used for reforestation.

Chipped elm for mulch

Diversity planting will produce a resilient and beneficial urban forest. With edible species in the mix, we can create an urban environment that is more food secure.

Oak, or other large nut trees

Currants

Lupines, or other nitrogen-fixing plants

Raspberries

Groundcovers

Edible herbs

Edible Ecosystem design for a bus stop.

Why Strip the Ecosystem?

When we develop new land, we tend to strip the landscape clean. We clear-cut forest for new farmland and bulldoze wild grasslands for new suburbs. We still are paving over the last remaining wild spaces in urban areas instead of instituting better land planning to meet infrastructure needs. Cities have almost completely replaced the former ecosystem with a new one. Unfortunately, the new one is less diverse, less beneficial, and less resilient.

The developers of this newly built hotel had the opportunity to integrate the natural landscape around it. Now they are offered another opportunity: the ability to create a diversified, edible ecosystem along walkways, parking lots, and courtyards. But will they take the opportunity?

Development Doldrums

The new development pictured here is in a rapidly growing community in Canada. The developers are following the standard land-planning paradigm of stripping the ecosystem away, laying out a grid, and then planting lawns and a few ornamental trees along roads and in front of houses. Behind the development, the remnant of the ecosystem tells a sad tale of what was lost. Here, a mix of species found in boreal and deciduous woodlands occurs as a biodiverse **ecotone** (edge of two biomes). There was wintergreen, sweet gale, Labrador tea, strawberry, red and sugar maples, red oak, aspen, white pine, black raspberries, red raspberries, chokecherries, alder, and much more.

One of the beautiful and aromatic plants stripped away was sweet gale. Just walking through a patch of sweet gale makes one feel at ease. Its flower tops and leaves can be used to make tea and will help with headaches, fevers, and rheumatisms.

Monoculture Land Planning/Management

Humans have increasingly changed over to monocultural land management. This is true for urban, rural, and suburban landscapes.

- **Urban:** limited diversity of city trees, greenspaces, and planters.
- **Rural:** monoculture farming and tree plantations
- **Suburban:** lawns and ornamental tree monocultures

We must allow diverse and mature ecosystems to return if we are to regain that highly productive mosaic of ecosystem successional stages that have always nurtured human societal success and community well-being.

Stagnation of Ecological Success

One of the consequences of monoculture in farms and cities is the prevention of ecosystems from developing complexity. It produces a stagnation of ecological succession by keeping farms and lawns in a perpetual state of early growth and evolution. The consequence is we don't garner the benefits of more mature ecological communities. For example, we do this by plowing in farm country and valuing mowed lawns in suburbia. We no longer allow cultural landscapes to return to mature ecosystems. We need land planning to conserve and regenerate mature wild spaces for multifunctional benefits and long-lasting potential.

Segregation of Habitat

One of the results of modernization is the segregation of our **foodscape*** from the communities where we live. Food is produced in one area, and people live in another. This is often referred to as the **urban-rural divide.** But this is also a disconnect of export and import between global resource regions. This has three main consequences: 1) we are unaware of the impact of our purchase choices on far-away environments; 2) we do not benefit from those ecosystems that are healthy, and 3) the source of our wealth and well-being is insecure because it is far away and we are only indirectly connected to it. *This is a habitat divided.*

* A landscape where food is produced, usually farmland.

Foodscape   Communities

In Sweden, lingonberries grow in woodlands, and they were traditionally harvested for jams and juices. When we harvest our own foods, we experience the environment they come from, when we nurture that environment near-to-home we enjoy its further benefits beside our communities.

Above: *We must see the whole as more than the sum of its parts. The Earth is a whole and dynamic system worthy of respect above and beyond human economies and science that depend on the whole.*

Top right: *We have segregated our human habitat. We no longer live surrounded by edible and diverse abundance. Instead, our land planning allocates some areas for neighborhoods and others for food production.*

Bottom right: *We are more accustomed to experiencing foods within a disconnected environment, namely the grocery store. Grocery stores do not shade our streets, clean our air and water, or produce the food we need. Our purchase choices can help get those things done—if they support regenerative practices near-to-home.*

Maximizing Multifunctional Services

Scientists and Traditional Ecological Knowledge (TEK) recognize and promote the value of ecosystem services. Ecosystems are multifunctional, with many useful goods and services. Our modern disconnection means we cannot benefit from the many ecosystem services that a healthy food-scape provides, and we cannot directly support these services. Biodiverse farmland, for instance, can help mitigate flooding downriver for adjacent neighborhoods. Here, the inclusion of edible hedges, riparian buffers, and intercropped perennial and annual production helps slow rainfall, reduces runoff, and improves soil water holding capacity.

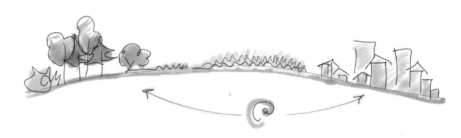

Modern
Ecosystem Services

*Let's **continue to zoom into** the western tip of the island of Montreal, Quebec, near the town of Sainte-Anne-de-Bellevue. Here there is a striking divide between urban and suburban (where most people live) and rural areas (where our food is produced and our resources extracted). Reconnecting this divided landscape and reinvigorating its ecosystem services for local communities is a powerful aim for the future.*

Goods and Services

Ecosystems have **goods and services** that benefit all creatures. Human society has always benefited from functioning ecosystems. Today, edible ecosystems in our communities can help slow rain and prevent stormwater surges that pollute our rivers and overwhelm sewage treatment. They can reduce the urban heat island effect by influencing microclimates, providing shade, and holding moisture in urban areas. They can reduce the use of pesticides in rural areas through improved pest management from diverse intercropping.

Four Major Services

Ecosystems services can be organized into four categories to help understand the immense value of our forests, wetlands, grasslands, and other ecologically complex landscapes.

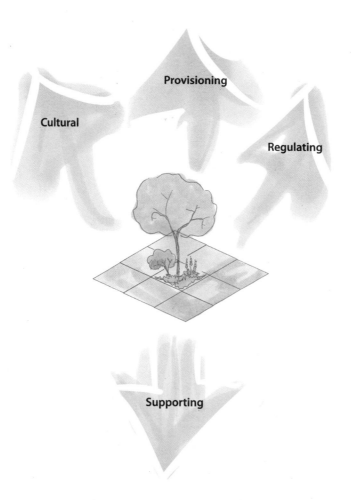

Whole System

Although we will discuss the four major categories of ecosystem services below and provide examples of each, it is important to remember ecosystem services function as a whole system. Indeed, that is very much the point. We need to support ecological functions within whole systems. Keep this in mind as we will look at ecosystem design in Section 3.

Edible ecosystems, such as a food forest, are very good at providing food, as well as producing oxygen, regulating climate, and improving soil. Food forests are designed as a whole system with diverse plant layers and relationships between air, soil, water, organisms, and people.

Provisioning

Provisioning services include fruits, vegetables, meats, clean water, fish, wood, and other goods that we enjoy and consume. Sometimes we refer to ecosystems as having goods and services—provisioning is the tangible ecological products (the goods). What is the value to society of food, water, and lumber? Whether grown on a farm, harvested in wild woodland, or provided by the sea, these are important ecosystem provisions on this life-raft planet in our universal sea. Whether the products come from a cultural or wild landscape, the ecosystem requires careful management in our modern world to ensure regenerative products and low impact on other ecosystem services.

Svenska Nyår

These delicious treats from a Swedish New Year's party have all been provided by ecosystems: jam from Scandinavian lingonberries, coffee from Guatemala, chocolate from Costa Rican cacao trees, wine made from Portuguese grapes, and wheat from the Ukraine for the cakes.

Regulatory

Regulatory services help keep our planetary systems in balance. They include purification of water, air, and soils, as well as flood mitigation, cooling of temperatures during heat waves, and carbon sequestration. Erosion control, for instance, is a regulatory service critical to agriculture, forestry, and city planning. Cities are seeing the value in maintaining healthy ecosystems upstream of their watersheds to make sure the water flowing into the city is clean and to prevent the need for excess siltation, fertilizer, and other contaminants to be removed using costly water purification technology.

Pollination is an ecosystem service that is critical for ecological functioning. Humans are dependent on pollination services for farms, orchards, market gardens, forestry, and landscaping. Around 85% of all plants on Earth require pollinator species.[14] Pollinators are responsible for many fruits, vegetables, herbs, and berries, as well as oil and fiber crops. Pollinator species include bees, birds, butterflies, moths, and beetles. According to the Pollinator Partnership, there are 180,000 plant species and 1,200 crops that require pollination. These services represent over 200 billion dollars in our global economy. Pollinator species are also fundamental to ecosystems and help support other benefits to humans by maintaining plant diversity and ecosystem productivity. A critical aspect of *The Edible Ecosystem Solution* is the creation and maintenance of pollinator habitat using the model presented in Section 4.

Cultural

Cultural services make our lives better by providing spaces for education, recreation, aesthetic beauty, and stewardship. We will discuss many of these services in more detail when we take a closer look at human wellness and education (see "Livable Community Benefits"), but they remain one of the more easily understood ecosystem services—we all enjoy a walk through the forest, fresh wild berries on the bush, and the sound of the birds.

Spending time outside, picking berries, and walking in wild spaces is good for our health, builds community spirit, and allows us to be surrounded by the wonderful wild aesthetic.

Supporting

Supporting services include many of the fundamental ecological productions that maintain ecosystem functioning and *support* the other services: cultural, regulating, and provisioning. Supporting services include photosynthesis, biodiversity, habitat, and soil formation. Let's look at soil formation.

Soil formation is an important part of natural resource management for farms, forestry, and other economies that are directly supported by soil. Ecosystems build soil through the decomposition by soil microorganisms of their leaf-fall, twigs, and root shedding. The biodiversity in a single teaspoon of soil is incredible. A gram of soil can contain billions of bacteria, yards of mycorrhizal fungi filaments, and thousands of protozoa. Soil life and quality soil are critical for the fixing, storing, cycling, and releasing of nutrients to plants. Biodiverse soil is more productive for crops and trees, stores more carbon to offset anthropogenic emissions, improves soil retention in floods, and helps hold water in droughts. Yes, the benefits for agriculture, forestry, landscaping, and climate change are immense.

Soil testing can be valuable to better understand which plants your soil can sustain and how to improve soil for enhanced productivity.

Big-Picture Services

Shall we go closer? *Ecosystems are essential for our societal well-being, then and now, and there are some ecosystem services that should be seen in relation to the big picture today. Now, let's zoom into the western tip of the island, where, like many urbanizing areas, flooding from climate change poses a risk to residents, and human well-being is under threat from development.*

Essential to Resilience

There are a few essential services ecosystems provide for societal resilience. Working to improve ecosystems is vital to allowing these big-picture services to achieve their potential. As we will see in Section 3, these big-picture services can be manifested in simple micro-landscapes, which, as discussed in Section 4, can be designed to catalyze a global paradigm shift. *The Edible Ecosystem Solution* is very much focused on maximizing these big-picture ecosystem services in an affordable and effective manner.

We are undermining the very foundation of our wealth and well-being through biodiversity loss and poor land-use planning.

We have been using up our natural capital at an alarming rate through degradation, fragmentation, and extinction of biodiversity. This includes cutting down forest for monocultures, such as soy or palm oil, and paving over prairies for more shopping centers—where they sell the same damn things as the shopping centers beside them.

Climate Change First of all, ecosystems, such as forest, woodlands, grasslands, and wetlands, are excellent carbon sinks. These ecosystems sequester, or pull, carbon out of the atmosphere and put it into their woody stems or store it in the soil as soil organic matter. The best solution to climate change for all of us to do right now is the simplest one: plant a tree or a small ecological landscape—a hedgerow on the farm or schoolyard. A single tree has an annual benefit of about $53,000 annually.[15] This estimate includes calculating the impact of the tree on increased property value, air quality control, energy savings, CO_2 reduction, and stormwater reduction.

Compared to the other climate solutions offered, planting trees is the simplest, most affordable, and most achievable solution right now. A large (6–8 foot) maple tree or fruit tree can be purchased for about $90. A bag of smaller trees (about 1 foot tall) can cost only .50 to $1 each. We can debate endlessly about reducing our use of fossil fuels and improving technologies and changing consumption patterns, but ultimately, while we are figuring all that out, let's plant trees in our communities, and let's make them high-impact trees.

High-impact trees are those that yield goods and services that are highly useful to the surrounding community; some produce fruits or nuts, with welcoming shade, and some yield regenerative harvests, like cinnamon or cork trees. Quick to produce and/or long-lived species are often high-impact; healthy and locally adapted varieties are *always* higher impact.

Banana trees readily grow in subtropical climates, such as this one in Guerrero, Mexico, and can produce heavy yields of nutritious food (around 30 pounds per stem). They also work well in steep terrain to manage water runoff and can even be used to maximize greywater in communities. High-impact trees quickly make a difference in a community and/or have a long-lasting effect.

Biodiversity Regeneration Ecosystems support biodiversity, and biodiversity supports ecosystems. We are at the start of a massive planetary extinction. If we don't do something about it, we will face a complete undermining of all the benefits of biodiversity. Biodiversity is the cornerstone of much of our economies, societal well-being, and environmental stability. If we don't conserve and regenerate biodiversity, we risk losing its benefits to us: pollinators species to food production, undiscovered cures to disease, and the solutions to digesting our massive heaps of garbage in landfills and pollution in oceans. Life has many solutions to offer us.

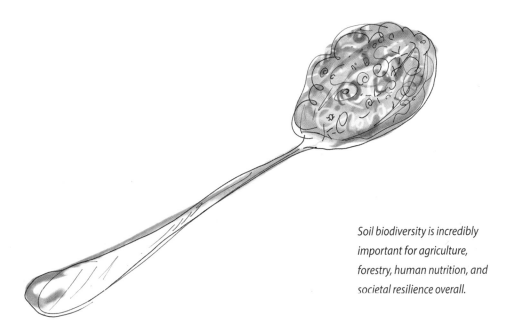

Soil biodiversity is incredibly important for agriculture, forestry, human nutrition, and societal resilience overall.

Ecosystem Healthcare Living a healthy lifestyle is critical to improving societal well-being. Humans need to spend more time outdoors, walking in wild spaces. We need to be eating fresher food, enjoying a more nutritious diet, breathing better air, drinking quality water, and tolerating less exposure to toxins in our environment. Ecosystems provide services that benefit us in all these ways. Vibrant ecosystems that are part of our communities can help us live better lives; being surrounded by wildness calms our nervous system, stimulates our minds and works our bodies. Healthy ecosystems clean our environment and improve access to fresh, nutritious foods through diversified land management. This is ecosystem healthcare.

Food security is having a cherry tree growing in your yard, community orchard, or laneway.

Food Security In 1996, the World Food Summit defined food security as "when all people at all times have access to sufficient, safe, nutritious food to maintain a healthy and active life." For us to achieve a food-secure world, we need to have food in our communities—where people live. We cannot depend on imported foods! Many of our necessary foods can be integrated into landscapes that prioritize edible and useful plants and local farms. Another aspect of food security is ensuring genetic diversity in food plants, so there is a large gene pool to draw upon for new varieties in the face of changing climates.

Soil Services Soil offers so many ecosystem services that 2015 was declared the International Year of Soils by the UN General Assembly. Healthy soil with a functioning soil food web and balanced composition can improve nutrients, water retention, pest management, and much more. The UN's declaration included highlighting soil's role in international food security, poverty alleviation, climate change mitigation, and providing overall essential societal benefits. Every micro-landscape is contributing to a global shift to a more resilient world through reconnecting the below-ground ecosystem with the above-ground biodiversity on which we depend.

We are affecting the fundamental life-support systems of our planet. Carbon emission into our atmosphere is altering the solar budget of our planet. Nutrient cycling is askew, with massive fertilizer, pesticide, and pollutant runoff, and outgassing that pours into our water and air. Biodiversity is being lost at a tremendous rate due to habitat fragmentation, pollution, and economic prioritizations.

We Pay for Ecosystem Services Indirectly

We pay for ecosystem services already. There are so many services that ecosystems provide that humans buy over the counter that could be had more affordably and efficiently right out our backyards.

Take essential oils, for instance. These high-value bottles of oils come from plants. The ingredients for many of the over-the-counter oils we buy for their health benefits can be grown in our front, back, and side yards. When I go outside in the spring, my nose is filled with the fragrance of peppermint, roses, lemon balm, and other wonderfully healthy scents. Conservation of wild space and designing edible ecosystems into our communities offers the essential oils—cheaply and much more enjoyable than mall shopping. The ponderosa forests of the North American West completely surround visitors with the rich scent of cinnamon and vanilla, an amazing scent to experience outside of the tropics.

The healthy benefits of various teas are well documented: improving human longevity, deepening sleep, enhancing concentration, aiding digestion, improving mood, and helping fight the common cold—another argument for surrounding ourselves with ecosystems that provide us with useful plants.

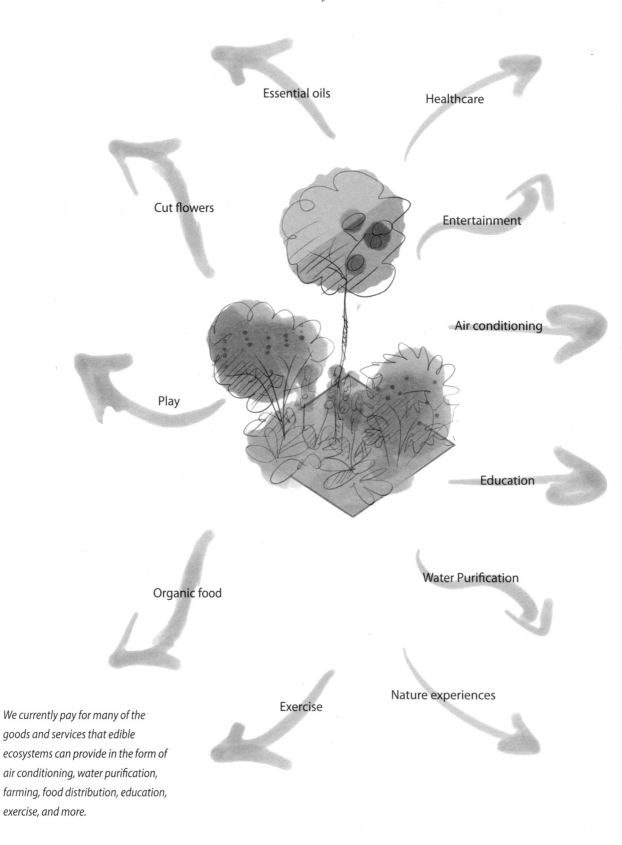

Essential oils

Healthcare

Cut flowers

Entertainment

Air conditioning

Play

Education

Organic food

Water Purification

Exercise

Nature experiences

We currently pay for many of the goods and services that edible ecosystems can provide in the form of air conditioning, water purification, farming, food distribution, education, exercise, and more.

Hidden Cost of Production

The food, lumber, medicines, cars, and toys we buy have hidden costs. These costs are not shown on the bottle and are rarely reflected in the price tag. This is because we are living off the dwindling resources of our planet through cheap, subsidized, and unsustainable modes of production across all industries.

The money moving around in this world that subsidizes poor production practices should be allocated to instituting **best management practices** for improving ecosystem services. Shopping, growing, and manufacturing locally helps reconnect us to the reality and consequences of our purchases.

Edible ecosystem landscapes put the mode of production in the face of the people who enjoy the products. We must take our ecological wealth in hand by revealing the cost of production and re-localizing our economies. Transitioning our landscapes is a critical stage in re-localizing our economies and building direct relationships with ecosystem goods and services.

Monoculture land use

Pollution of atmosphere

Over-consumption of finite resource

$4.99

Fragmentation of wildlife habitat

Poor working conditions/pay and loss of food sovereignty

Pollution of lakes, rivers, and ocean

Our products should have an ingredient list that includes what has been lost, and the price tag should reflect the immense value of ecosystem services being degraded.

Integrate Services into Communities

Our society would achieve immense benefit from integrating these services into our communities and supporting ecological functions through biodiversity. Especially important is the integration of the services of edible ecosystems. Since we already benefit from ecosystem services, it would be beneficial to have ecological landscapes near to our homes—where we can benefit more directly and be able to steward them. Communities with ecosystem landscapes would be actively helping achieve the "big-picture" services that local and planetary communities need. Edible ecological spaces are arguably still our best habitat.

Opportunities

Here in this community, not far from Montreal, Quebec, there are many opportunities for change. Let's take one of these neighborhoods and continue to zoom in. Here, like everywhere, greenspaces are underutilized; they are like a blank page full of potential for diversification. Uniform and organized, most of our greenspaces are ready to be reworked for change.

Greenspace Opportunities

Let's examine the types of greenspaces in modern communities and how they are poised for efficient and affordable transition to edible ecosystem landscapes. There is an abundance of uniform and organized, underutilized, and inefficient greenspaces across our landscapes. Some of our discussion on modern land use points out what is lacking in our communities, such as diversity, but rather than seeing these facts as negatives, I see them as opportunities for positive change. When you have room to improve, you can!

Whether a square of suburban lawn or the oldest city park in the Americas (the Palacio de Bellas Artes in Mexico City), there is an abundance of opportunities everywhere for enhancing community biodiversity. From replacing monoculture grass to planting areas of bare soil, our cultural landscapes are ready to integrate ecosystem services into communities.

Uniform Spaces

Most greenspaces in our modern communities are uniform. There are a limited number of types, sizes, and shapes of greenspace. In many suburban areas, there are yards, street medians, and parks. Urban areas include tree strips, large parks, and waterfronts. And on farms, there are fields, roads, and fence lines. Essentially, we are talking about spaces that are small, medium, or large, and they are primarily squares or rectangles (often long, linear rectangles—reminiscent of the shape of a garden bed). When we break it down, we see the opportunity for each space and the applicability of standard design practice.

In our modern world, there is an abundance of underutilized, organized, and uniform space.

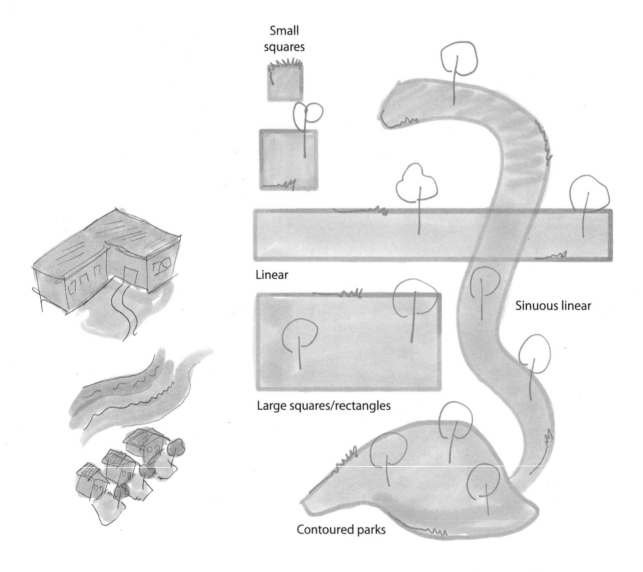

Small squares

Linear

Large squares/rectangles

Sinuous linear

Contoured parks

Types of Greenspaces

Small Squares/Rectangles This includes yards in most urban and suburban neighborhoods and towns. There are many other small, square or squarish shapes scattered throughout our modern landscape, including the planters and planted street corners that show up in some neighborhoods and business districts.

These small, square lawns with a view of Stockholm's famous Gamla Stan neighborhood are already organized to transition to different edible ecosystem spots that could serve to educate the many local and regional tourists about edible landscape potential in Scandinavia.

Large Squares/Rectangles This includes large parks, farms, and the grounds of public buildings and institutions, such as universities.

Large rectangular greenspace in downtown Kansas City.

Linear This includes medians, sidewalk edges, riversides, and fronts of businesses and institutions. Consider the front of this government building downtown Ottawa.

Left: *This school has a large square greenspace, but the fence line is a linear space with the opportunity for an edible hedge that can also serve as a privacy screen. This linear space used for fruit, berries, and herbs doesn't detract from the use of the yard for sport; it is underutilized space.*

Below: *This incredible waterfront trail system in Stockholm is a long linear greenspace that could be replanted to include a more diverse, edible, and useful understory—especially since it is currently under redevelopment!*

Underutilized and Inefficient

Most greenspaces in society are underutilized. They occupy only one or a few ecosystem layers, they don't cycle waste, and they have limited diversity and natural regeneration capabilities. When we maximize the space in our cultural landscape, we can increase the yield per square meter, or per acre, or per city block. The following illustrates the underutilized and inefficient nature of our modern greenspaces:

Limited Ecosystem Layers By layering a production space, we can increase net primary productivity, leading to an increase in photosynthesis and carbon sequestration. Most treed streets have only two layers in the ecosystem: trees and grass. We would receive myriad benefits of ecosystems with layered form and function.

Similar to the intricacy of architecture (seen in the famous Painted Ladies houses in San Francisco), our landscapes can be designed for maximizing ecosystem layers for ecological services—and be beautiful to behold, too.

Limited Diversity Most cultural landscapes have limited diversity. Farmland is primarily composed of a mosaic of a half dozen crops grown in monoculture acreage. The majority of suburban areas are made up of lawns and a select few ornamental trees and shrubs. Urban areas are predominately planted with popular shade trees. This makes us highly vulnerable to the spread of disease and pests, both of which are costly to manage.

Outbreaks of Dutch elm disease, pine bark beetle, and the emerald ash borer provide us with a cautionary tale of limited tree diversity in cities and our increasing vulnerability to change in our Earth's climate. The potato famine of Ireland is a good cautionary tale against monoculture agriculture.

When Broadway and many other streets were planted across Winnipeg in the late 1800s and early 1900s, they were mostly planted with a single tree species. The beautiful avenue, seen here circa 1910, is now threatened by Dutch elm disease, and, like many cities that planted monocultures, the urban canopy is in jeopardy. Photo courtesy of Manitoba Archives

Output/Input Dynamics Most greenspaces neglect the input/output dynamics necessary for a regenerative system. Most outputs (such as leaf-fall or fruit set) are seen as wastes, and costly inputs are brought in. Instead, for example, leaf-fall should be seen as a source of fertility and soil stability that would improve greenspace in the long term.

This row of young trees in Johannesburg, South Africa, have all their leaf-fall completely removed (and the grass clippings too). The cost of fertilizer and irrigation could be offset by managing leaf-fall as an input.

Natural Regeneration Most greenspaces have little-to-no natural regeneration. The presence of pervasive lawn and its regular mowing prevents tree seeds from finding fertile ground and growing to be a new layer in the ecosystem.

Despite the size of these trees in Beijing, there is no space for them to drop seed and naturally regenerate. Along with the immense investment China has put into reforestation, by developing a natural regeneration plan, they would get a leg up on future plantings and improve forest genetic diversity.

Planned Succession Despite a needed succession of urban and suburban greenspaces, there is little-to-no planted tree succession in our modern greenspaces. Most large city trees are only replaced when they die—which means an area goes from big trees to small trees, and there may be a lag period of having no trees. Growing the next canopy in the shade of the first is a natural principle that builds resilience into our urban and suburban greenspaces.

Brown Space Communities are full of brown space that isn't growing anything. The amount of brown space in your average city park, university quadrangle, and other so-called greenspaces is staggering. The edges of the pre-set paths are not buffered against surplus traffic and are compacted to the point of suppressing any green growth. Excessive mowing and drought can result in fragile sod being killed-off in patches. In farmland that floods easily, when it is compacted from heavy tillage, the result is large water-logged dead zones in the growing season.

Grey Space There is also an abundance of unnecessarily paved spaces in cities and suburbs. We can lift unneeded pavement, and plant trees. By prioritizing every square foot, and making more room for soil, we can gain the services provided by trees and edible landscapes in areas that would otherwise exist as unnecessary, dead stone. One key benefit of having more soil in the urban landscape is that it is capable of slowing, sinking, and storing water—improving urban greenspace and reducing runoff pollution.

Many greenspaces are going brown due to the monoculture management paradigm.

There are still many spaces that are simply unplanted, such as these planters in downtown Ottawa, Ontario. Brown space also occurs on farms where poor germination, erosion, and plant death result in bare ground.

Small Edges Make Big Plants We often overlook the little spaces in our landscapes. For instance, in urban areas, there are many cracks between paving, against walls, or at the edges where fences meet roads. These narrow spaces may have good soil underneath, and a little seed can stimulate productive results.

This profusion of cosmos in Montreal is growing from a two-inch crack in back-alley paving.

This rural road bordering a dairy farm near Guelph, Ontario, had but one old tree. Our current paradigm for treating these areas is as spaces that simply need to be maintained free of weeds, but the fence line between farm field and road is an ideal area for an edible hedge of fruit and nut trees and a berry understory, as shown in the sketch. When planted as edible landscape, these edges can provide community food security and farm business opportunities.

Organized Space Everywhere

Modern greenspaces are very organized. The "little boxes" of land-planned cities, suburbs, and countryside exist because it was an easy way for humans to think about landscape management. With a change of thinking, this same simplicity could lend itself to an efficient transition to edible ecosystems. Think of yards as bite-sized chunks of landscape to transition one at a time, each to showcase a formula for transitioning others.

Yes, we need more greenspace in communities. However, when we consider the inefficiency and underutilization of the spaces we already have—there is actually space everywhere!

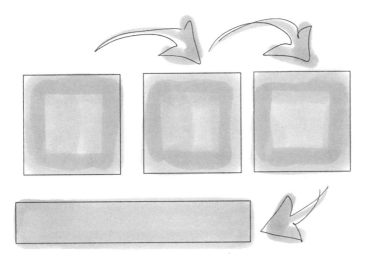

Winnipeg is actually quite a green city. It has many parks, medians, large yards, and lots of street tree spots. It is transition-ready to a diverse and edible ecological land pattern.

Transition-Ready!

The greenspaces in modern neighborhoods, public areas, and farms are **transition-ready landscapes**—blank pages for edible landscaping. Because our greenspaces are so organized and uniform, it would be relatively easy to convert them to edible ecological abundance. In the countryside, farms are already all laid out for the integration of trees along fence lines; in the suburbs, walking trails could include fruit and berries; in city parks, edible hedges could easily be planted to surround big, grassy spaces.

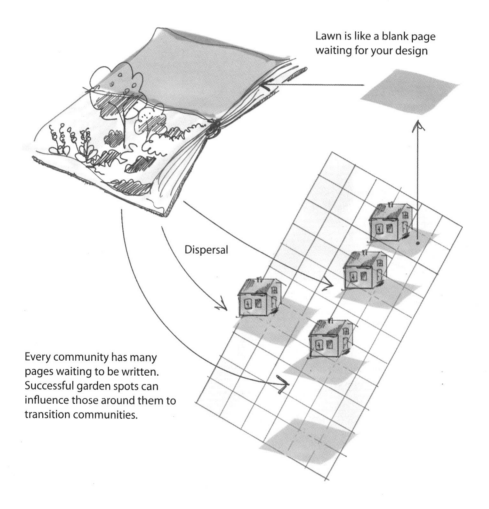

Lawn is like a blank page waiting for your design

Dispersal

Every community has many pages waiting to be written. Successful garden spots can influence those around them to transition communities.

Transition-ready spaces are stewardship opportunities; one garden spot can influence other spots. These transition-ready landscapes can include yards, parks and businesses, universities, colleges and schools, as well as farms, medians, greenways, and much more.

City Parks

City parks are one of the few greenspaces left in some urban areas. I find city parks interesting on several counts. First, it is ironic that many city parks used to be quarries or landfills (or both). Also, many desirable neighborhoods have been built around these former dumpsites turned greenspace. There wouldn't be so much greenspace remaining in cities if it weren't for these retrofitted quarries/dumping grounds. Maximizing spaces like these, as well as our cemeteries and the no-man's-lands of large, interstate roundabouts, is key to improving our habitat.

Central Park

What would New York City be without Central Park? Central Park! Yet, even in the heart of one of the greatest cities—where greenspaces are at a premium—there is an abundance of **transition-ready space.** There are many opportunities for integrating edible and useful plants and maximizing ecosystem services in Central Park. What would this look like?

Part of Current Layout

Let's consider how we could maximize the value of Central Park to its community. We could do this by integrating an edible landscape into the existing layout, without disrupting its organizational framework for maintenance. For instance, the many walking trails and bike lanes throughout the park are common landscape lines in most cities; these are ideal for edible ecosystem design. The design, installation, and maintenance of linear plantings is straightforward and can be done with much of the same equipment and staff. For instance, park work crews can prepare and plant sites with standard shovels, rakes, and compost. Also, typical mowing equipment can be used to maintain the edges of the linear planting in much the same way as staff maintain existing walkway edges. By planting along the park's current layout lines, edible ecosystem benefits are better achieved as part of the park's usual management.

Costs

The cost to install edible landscapes in parks is quite reasonable and is no more than the money spent on other landscape redesigns and rejuvenations. Central Park has recently had a section of park undergoing a multi-million-dollar rejuvenation that primarily entailed mulching large trees, laying new sod, and repaving the walkway; that money would have gone further if it included an edible ecosystem install. Edible ecosystems provide far more benefits than sod and concrete, and they will provide for us for many generations.

Multifunctional Edible Fences

Ecosystems are inherently multifunctional; remember a simple edible landscape can produce food, clean air, and provide shade, etc. However, additional functions can be achieved when edible ecosystems are designed into a modern landscape to enhance other societal needs. For instance, in Central Park, the big grassy lawns are retired in springtime to allow grass regeneration and reduce foot traffic during vulnerable stage of spring growth. By integrating edible landscapes as hedges along walkways, a landscape is produced that is easy to manage and provides a natural barrier between pedestrian through-traffic and park leisure space.

In place of the purchase, maintenance, and seasonal install/removal cost of fences, install edible hedges can exclude people, and directing them, instead, through gates designed into the hedge landscape. The costs of a fence (purchase, seasonal installation, inevitable repairs, and replacement) is replaced by those of a multifunctional edible hedge with potential of short and long-term benefits, such as providing food, beauty, shade, and serving as an understory and future regeneration for older park trees to enhance urban forest resilience. Also, many park trees near laneways have extreme compaction around their trunk base, reducing nutrient and water uptake, slowing root growth, and affecting a tree's overall longevity. By integrating the space between existing lane-side trees with edible hedges, we would prevent accidental, but no less harmful, damage to the soil area from heavy traffic that goes off the footpaths. Again, we achieve more value from limited urban greenspace by maximizing underutilized and organized areas as an opportunity for better land management and community well-being.

Typical park walkways and fences are transition-ready spaces for edible ecosystem design.

Older trees
without
understory

Temporary exclusion fence

Vulnerable spring lawn

This fence is installed and taken down every year and is easy to hop over. Although there is nothing inherently wrong with this fence system, an edible landscape approach to management here has more benefits, offering fresh food, beautiful foliage, fragrant flowers, and pedestrian exclusion. Furthermore, it would be a highly prized tourist attraction for this city park and all others, appealing to the interest and growing concern about our food, environment, and community health.

Bike lanes and walkways within Central Park are uniform, organized, and underutilized, and so opportune for integrating multifunctional edible hedges to prevent soil compaction, improve lawn health, and advance ecosystem services overall.

Livable
Community Benefits

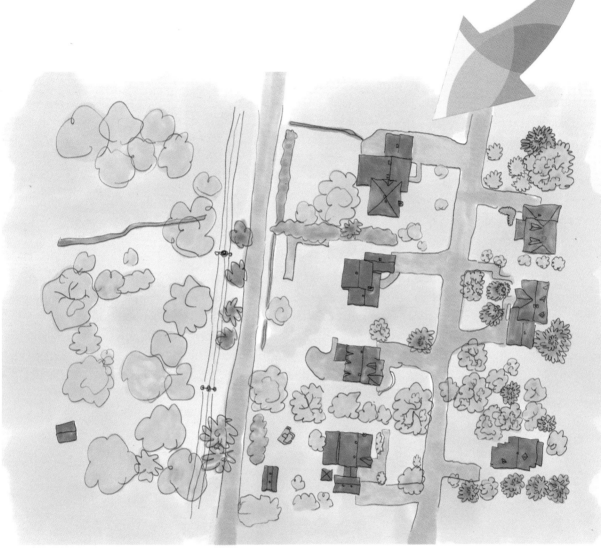

A bird's eye view of this street shows the homes of people living their lives. Yet, perhaps a livable community should include access to ecological education, homegrown remedies, improved well-being, and green jobs (local food production, for example).

Land, People, and a Plan: We Are Ready!

It is not just the land that is transition-ready. The current **healthy living and eco-conscious zeitgeist** has us prepped for simple hands-on action. We are itching for something straightforward to *do*. The edible ecosystem solutions, presented here, can be employed by anyone, anywhere, in any small spot! What is more, we can build a more enjoyable, healthy, prosperous, and resilient community.

Where you spend most of your time is your habitat. Your daily paths are opportunities for rejuvenation. A bit of edible ecosystem in our yards along the paths we travel every day can provide for human necessities and well-being.

A Look at Livable Communities

Communities are judged on their safety, recreational spaces, access to grocery stores, and other conveniences. For some, communities are about the connection with people who live in the neighborhood and the quality of relationships formed. Still further, we might consider the jobs available nearby so we can have meaningful occupation without a long commute. Ultimately, a livable community should provide the necessities of life and improve human well-being.

*Our bodies are built to interact with wild spaces. Our ancestors evolved in wild ecosystems, and we are at ease and healthy in them; whether we are running or picking fruit, wild spaces nourish us. How accessible is the connection to well-being in your community and other services that make it **livable?***

Better-Quality Community Greenspace

Having more greenspace—and better-quality greenspaces—makes communities more livable. Ecosystem-designed landscapes provide high-quality recreational opportunities, fresh food, and a clean environment. Here, an environment rich in colors, scents, and sights draws in neighbors to pick fruit together and enjoy meaningful contact with each other and the ecosystem. In low-income neighborhoods, this transformation is a positive impact on food security; and everywhere, this results in community resilience and societal well-being. The underutilized space in our urban, suburban, and rural communities is low-quality when compared with the **ecosystem services of biodiversity.**

Communities should be healthy, happy, and meet people's needs as directly as possible. Fresh food, fewer toxins, green jobs, and recreation are a few benefits of edible ecosystem greenspaces.

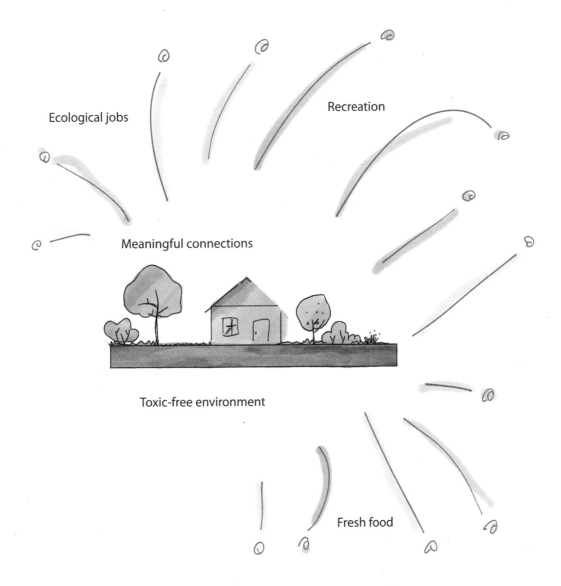

Ecosystem Education

A child's mind is a sponge—absorbing experiences to inform their life. Children are the next generation of leaders, and their education is formative to our future societal successes. Today, few children can say *where broccoli comes from, or what a cherry tree looks like.* They are disconnected from seasonal cycles and the care of biodiversity—despite its fundamental role in human origin and our future societal resilience. **Ecosystems are sorely missed educational opportunities.** Classroom experiments, like growing sunflower sprouts in egg cartons, are only twigs in the branching neurological activity stimulated in children from wild, edible, and biodiverse landscapes. Exposure to edible ecosystems in yards, schools, and public spaces can also result in wider knowledge, such as the mathematics of fruit yield, or poetry about blossoming trees. Also, these spaces provide closer intimacy and knowledge of food with ripples into diet and overall childhood health, which can improve academic performance. This educational approach can be implemented on university grounds, where student cognitive activity and academic completion could be improved with rest and rejuvenation in biodiverse landscapes, and living laboratories could offer hands-on experiences. Finally, let's remember that our sciences, mathematics, arts—and everything else we deem an incredible intellectual achievement of humankind—were first inspired by diverse natural systems.

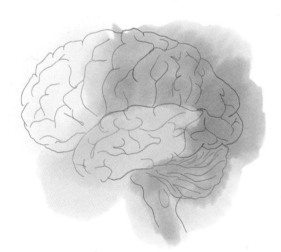

Edible ecosystems are stimulating environments for the mind. Many of our best thinkers retreat to the woods to work in their thought sanctuaries. Research has shown that time around birds, bees, flowers, and trees improves our mental clarity and helps us be more productive.

Green Jobs

Prioritizing more edible ecosystem abundance in our communities can also open new "green" job opportunities in every neighborhood. Global, regional, and local economies are underpinned by employment. It is about time we rebuild our economies through employment in work that improves our community well-being and societal resilience. There are many professional opportunities that can support biodiversity for local and global benefit, including market gardening, landscape design, arboriculture, compost management, and nurseries, as well as specialized work within city planning, landscape architecture, and research. Nay-sayers may point out that there will be increased work in the maintenance of a more diverse landscape. However, we already invest in city landscape maintenance, and we could have a higher return of valuable goods and services from our cultural landscape by shifting some of these costs to more biodiverse landscape maintenance. It would be an excellent investment in our future.

Ecosystems provide financial benefits such as goods to sell and services that reduce our food, healthcare, and other expenses. Green jobs build soil carbon, reduce pollution, and improve food security. Edible cities are a tourism opportunity that shouldn't be overlooked, for it will soon be readily booked. Community well-being and societal resilience can underpin our economy through edible ecosystem employment.

Harvest is an age-old way of getting physical excercise and community food sales provide food security.

Urban and suburban agriculture is a "green job" of the future that prioritizes feeding people in their own communities and maintaining greenspace, so it doesn't get paved over. Diversified urban farms provide other ecosystem services to their communities because they are near to the consumers.

Abundant fruit in your yard saves money, green jobs make money, and transitioning land to edible ecological abundance builds financial wellness for individuals, communities, and society.

Measuring Quality of Life

How do we measure quality of life in our communities? Quality of life includes who you are, your current circumstances, and the wider environment. Consider how you live your life and the capacity of a more diverse landscape to improve your quality of life.

Let's look at it this way: Where you are, what you eat, and how you spend your time is who you are. Many of us live busy lives, surrounded by concrete and immersed in technology. We purchase old, denatured, diluted, substituted, and even artificial foods. We turn to aromatherapy, weekends away, and organic food stores, yet these are band-aids for the truly human experience of community, living surrounded by fresh food, spending time together outside picking berries, sharing skills, and helping each other thrive.

This typical neighborhood could provide a higher quality of life.

Communities with diverse ecosystems are much healthier for humans and enrich our bodies, minds, and spirit.

What makes a space livable? For the majority of human existence, having food near-to-home was critical. This Stockholm neighborhood would be more livable if fresh harvests of fruit, nuts, berries, and herbs were available seasonally.

Is there anything more human than walking along a berry path, picking fresh fruits—enjoying the flavors now and later—talking with friends under the sun, having your feet on the ground, and sharing and receiving diverse richness through an exchange of products and stories?

Well-being is Multifaceted

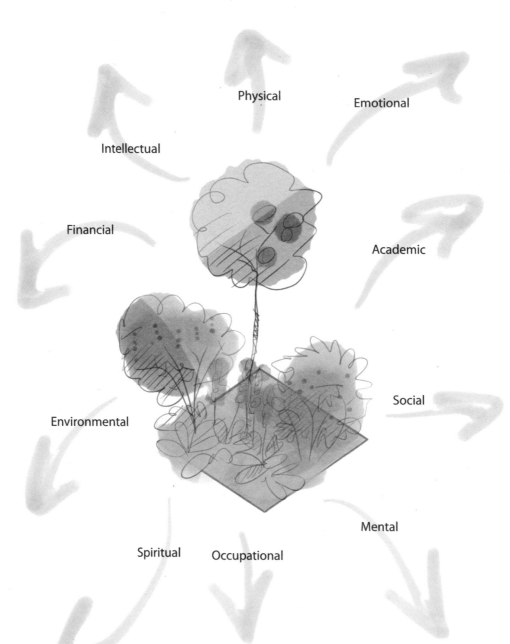

Physical

Emotional

Intellectual

Financial

Academic

Environmental

Social

Mental

Spiritual   Occupational

*Well-being is multifaceted, and edible ecosystems contribute
to each of these sectors!*

What Is Health to Societal Success?

"Health" can refer to mental, emotional, physical, or spiritual states of being. One of the best things we can do for our health is to have a healthy lifestyle, including proper nutrition, exercise, and living in a clean environment. To this end, many doctors have started prescribing walks outside, ideally in wild spaces. Being healthy is a big part of our happiness, our sense of well-being, and our capacity to be confident. When we are healthy, work gets done, children are cared for, friendships are made, and we make meaningful contributions to society. Health is the cornerstone of individual and societal productivity.

Fresh berries from a typical food forest design in a suburban yard improve well-being.

Edible ecosystem gardens provide fresh food to this suburban home, including a micro-landscape spot with corn, beans, and squash tucked up against the house, and a macro-landscape for a front yard. The macro-landscape is a 300-foot-long edible hedge that includes nitrogen-fixing trees and shrubs, raspberries, currants, asparagus, and strawberries, as well as pollinator habitat and several mature trees that are integrated with the new understory; namely a heritage apple, and native white oaks.

Ecological Healthcare

Biodiverse landscapes reduce environmental toxins and improve beneficial outputs such as fresh fruits, wonderful scents, and beautiful sights, all of which are beneficial to health. Proximity to diverse ecosystems, eating a variety of foods, and getting outdoor exercise can improve our gut flora; the diversity in our intestines is critical for good digestion and the prevention of disease. Research shows that a diverse diet leads to diversity in our microbiome and can help prevent obesity, diabetes, and inflammatory bowel syndrome.[16] Living in a cleaner environment and eating fresh foods also results in lower levels of toxins in humans, which pose risks to cognitive development and physical functioning, and can result in IQ deficits.[17] Ecological healthcare has increasingly been studied, in particular by followers of *shinrin yoku*.* Research shows that time spent in wilder spaces reduces anxiety, depression, and stress, and it improves mood, focus, and sleep. Research also shows that outdoor time boosts natural killer cells that help your immune system fight cancer and promotes speedier recovery from illness.[18] Although the study of edible ecosystems is in its beginning stages at this time, the benefits of healthy eating and time in wild spaces will certainly translate to higher **ecological healthcare**. We are our ecosystem and environment!

* This means "forest bathing," which is the practice of spending time in natural spaces. It was developed as a healthcare practice in Japan in the 1980s, based on the profound benefits of being in wild spaces.[19]

"Climb the mountains and get their good tidings. Nature's peace will flow into you as sunshine flows into trees. The winds will blow their own freshness into you, and the storms their energy, while cares will drop away from you like the leaves of Autumn."

— John Muir[20]

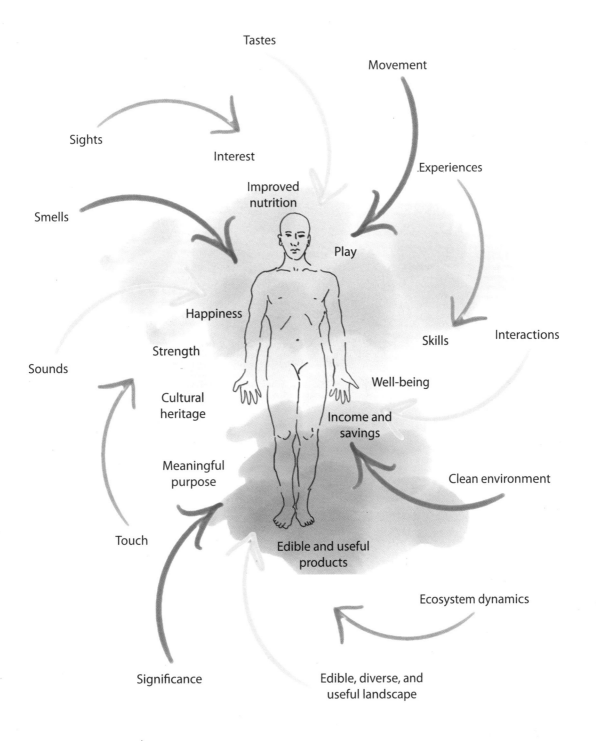

Tastes
Movement
Sights
Interest
Experiences
Improved nutrition
Smells
Play
Happiness
Skills
Interactions
Strength
Well-being
Sounds
Cultural heritage
Income and savings
Meaningful purpose
Clean environment
Touch
Edible and useful products
Significance
Ecosystem dynamics
Edible, diverse, and useful landscape

"Short exposures to nature can make us less aggressive, more creative, more civic minded and healthier overall."
— Florence Williams [21]

Our overall evolutionary structure is based in wild diversity. Biodiversity still nourishes our ancestral body, mind, and spirit.

Nutritious Food

Foods that are fresher are more nutritious, and meals composed of fruits and vegetables with diverse colors have more diversity of nutrition. Wild foods are also bringing more diversity to our diet and are full of important micronutrients that our bodies love. Although there are hundreds of thousands of edible plants in the world, humans today eat only about 200 different food plants. We need to get more food locally and from within our communities. Local food is fresher, has direct relationships to your community land and watershed management, and is certainly an opportunity to get out and enjoy local greenspace by shopping on the farm or growing it in our own yards.

There are so many foods we can grow in our yards and public greenspaces to diversify our diets. Diversity of food is important for our health and a joyous culinary experience.

Chinese herbs are so diverse. A visit to a Chinese "farmacy" yielded over 80 different plant medicines in their whole plant form.

Hospital Greenspaces

Imagine if, in 1960, when this photo was taken of the Winnipeg General Hospital, this large expansive lawn (at the time heavily managed with herbicides and regularly mowed) had been planted instead into diversified fruit, berries, herbs, and medicinals! Now, there would be a 60-year-old edible ecosystem for patients to enjoy; they could sit and recover in the dappled shade, eat fresh fruits for the cafeteria, and welcome the rejuvenating view from the windows. What's more—this is a children's hospital! Let's not let time slip by us again! We should be maximizing our greenspaces for ecological healthcare near hospitals, retirement homes, and other health institutions.

Children's Hospital   *Winnipeg General Hospital, 1960*

Photo credit: Archives of Manitoba

Craving Ecosystems

Today, we are craving the wild. Research shows that natural spaces calm our nervous system, reduce anxiety and depression, and improve productivity and focus. Time spent in the wild shows marked increases in the hormone dopamine, enhancing our mood, critical thinking, and decision-making capacity, as well as the functioning of our immune system. Our habitats should nourish every part of us as individuals and communities and as a prosperous society.

Ecosystems provide habitat for endangered species and outdoor educational opportunities for our children, with long-term benefits for cognitive development.

Common Lines

As we zoom into the edges between properties, streets, and homes, the common lines in our neighborhoods come into focus as the graph paper for livable community benefits. As we get closer to where we live, let's quicken the pace of zooming in. Here, we zoom into the edges.

Lines in the Landscape

In all communities, whether urban, rural, or suburban, there are *lines* in our landscape. If we change our thinking a little bit, we will see these lines are everywhere: they are the roads we drive, the edges of properties, our fence lines, and many other linear landscape features. Humans have always gridded their landscape, so these lines abound.

Common Lines

We have developed landscapes in much the same way everywhere; one of the results is *common lines*. If we look at a dozen houses situated on different pieces of land, we can see many common lines. Each has a property front onto a sidewalk, a driveway edge, a perimeter fence, a back hedge, and the outline of the house's footprint. A fence line or driveway, etc., is here termed a common line, because most communities have these landscape features, and these are very often associated with bits of underutilized space. They are edges, and edges are often neglected. These common lines in our communities represent opportunities for transitioning our landscape into edible ecosystems. They also serve as a template for showcasing how to transition other properties with similar common lines. Indeed, what we all have in common is a more-or-less universal community layout and the benefit in common of turning this into edible biodiversity.

The Space Between

One of the most basic ways we can integrate diversity into our communities is by planting the space between our street trees. With this ecological connect-the-dot, we can make a more beautiful, productive, and healthy community picture. Not only are these spaces underutilized, they are also inefficient to manage. It takes much more work to mow around trees than it does to mow a straight strip along each side of an edible hedge in which the large street trees form the canopy with berry bushes, shrubs, and herbs forming the understory.

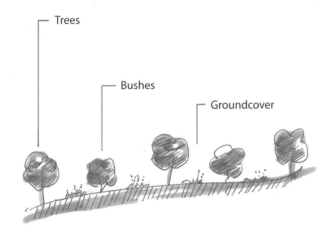

Alternating the form/size of different edible and useful species creates a diversified and organized edible hedgerow.

The common lines of this waterfront in North Bay, Ontario, are just waiting for a long, edible hedgerow. These lines are transition-ready and occur in many spaces, like edges of properties, walkways, bike lanes, and tree rows.

The layout of this row of street trees in Winnipeg's Osborne Village is well lined up for biodiverse under-plantings in the space between older street trees.

Micro-Landscapes

This view of the front yard shows how common lines delineate opportunities for edible ecosystem abundance in the margins of daily existence. We do this through the development of micro-landscapes that can fit into our transition-ready spaces, no matter the size.

Different micro-landscapes can easily be designed as edible ecosystems.

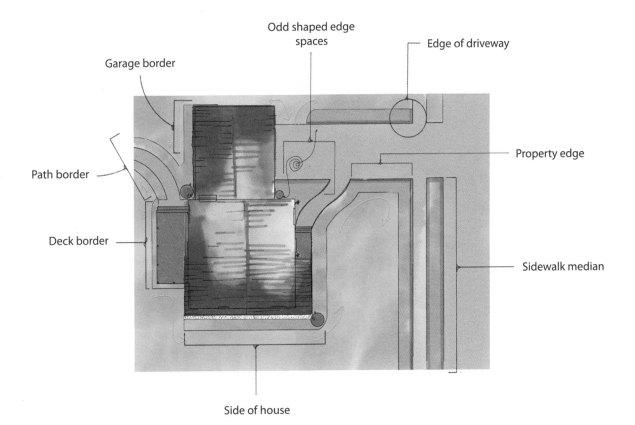

Garage border

Odd shaped edge spaces

Edge of driveway

Path border

Deck border

Property edge

Sidewalk median

Side of house

A Piece of Land

Essentially, a micro-landscape is a portion of landscape within a larger greenspace: it could be a patch of backyard just 5' by 5', an entire property front, or the length of a pathway's edge in a city park. It is a piece of land, and together with many other pieces makes up the whole landscape in any community. If you own a property, you are sure to have many micro-landscapes where your greenspaces meet the type of common lines just discussed. Human habitat transition starts with micro-landscapes.

These bits of lawn have little utility for sports or leisure and are mostly a hassle to mow and maintain. Yet with edible ecosystem design, we could have a garden plot, an orchard spot, or an herb row. Micro-landscapes can brighten the community and improve the property owner's access to life-giving ecosystem goods and services.

This turn-of-the-century home has several micro-landscapes, seen as distinct greenspaces: the polygon shape to the left of the sidewalk and the lawns on either side of the stairway and the median. You could even call the little strip in front of the retaining wall a micro-landscape. Wouldn't it be wonderful to have strawberries or chamomile planted there?

Landscape or Ecosystem?

Ecosystems can easily fit into the various spaces available for micro-landscapes. But first, the difference between *a garden*, an *edible landscape*, and an *edible ecosystem* must be examined. Gardens are familiar features in rural areas and part of the growing food movement in urban spaces as well. Gardens often contain annual* vegetables planted that are harvested each year. The yield of a garden is high in calories, but the management and inputs are also relatively high, requiring yearly turning over of the soil, fertilization, new crop plantings, and compost waste management.

On the other hand, an edible landscape is more akin to the landscaping we see done in front of businesses and homes (usually with flowers or ornamental shrubs), but, in this case, primarily using perennial** food plants instead. Edible landscapes have less annual maintenance than gardens because upfront costs of planting long-lasting berry bushes and/or fruit trees pay off with less annual labor over the lifespan of the bush or tree. For instance, trees are more robust in droughts once they get their roots into the soil, whereas vegetables require weekly watering in dry spells. Edible landscapes are also more forgiving if you go away for a week or two, or even take a year off from management, still returning yields in future years with minimal reinstated care.

The difference between an *edible landscape* and an *edible ecosystem* is mostly a question of **ecosystem mimicry** that results in less maintenance and more resilience—remember, ecosystems are diverse and have layered form and multiple functions. A forest is made of many trees, bushes, ferns, flowers, animals, fungi, and soil biota that stretch across a landscape. This biodiversity helps maintain soil fertility, regulate disease cycles, and improve the whole system's resilience and productivity. Landscaping to *mimic* this form and function is **edible ecosystem design**.

So, whereas an edible landscape may consist of planting a few chosen fruit trees in your yard, an edible ecosystem will consist of fruit trees, berry bushes, herbs, and groundcovers planted as a whole unit, and all will be suitable to your local soil and climate. The wild and diversified nature of an edible ecosystem means the micro-landscape is more independent of human care. They provide habitat for beneficial insects and regulate fertility, organic matter, and water while self-propagating their various plant components naturally—and all the while offering meaningful products for human use, and a beautiful yard to boot.

* Annual plants regrow from seed each year, whether wild or cultivated.

** Perennials are plants live for more than two years, and return each year to grow larger, such as a tree.

Micro-Topography

We looked at how ecosystems change and merge across a landscape in response to differences in climates, terrain, soil, and moisture availability. We can also consider the effects of unique circumstances that occur only in smaller areas. Consider micro-topography in your yard. Where does water collect? Where are there raised and dry mounds? You can take advantage of these unique conditional issues and enhance them using ecosystem design. In doing so, you can help foster micro-ecosystems, achieving ecosystem benefits in the small spaces available for micro-landscapes.

A single spot can serve as a rain garden to help with stormwater.

Micro-Ecosystem

An ecosystem, edible or not, can be defined at any scale. Below is a picture of colonies of fungi living solely within a hollow log, with spiders and other insects eating and living there. This log is also nursing a young hemlock tree with ferns growing at its margins and mosses and lichens growing on its surfaces. The hollow, wet ground at its base is home to a salamander. This whole thing is a micro-ecosystem.

Ecosystems Are Scalable

Yet, this log can also be seen as being part of another ecosystem—a component of the whole. The woodland in which the log lies is also an ecosystem. In the same way, a landscaped spot of yard can be an edible ecosystem within a landscaped property—which is also an ecosystem within an entire neighborhood's ecosystem. This interconnected nature is, as this book will show, *the* chief strength in creating change in our modern landscapes. Yes, ecosystems are interconnected, and also they expand to fill available space, naturally and with human care.

The influence of this log as an ecosystem can grow outward and change as the log rots. The ferns, fungi, and mosses will spread, the hemlock will grow to become a canopy tree, and the salamanders can multiply. The log itself is one of many logs in the forest inhabited by similar but different micro-ecosystems.

Full-Service Micro-Landscapes

Micro-ecosystems provide a complete complement of *provision, regulating, supporting,* and *cultural services,* similar to larger ecosystems and biomes. They sequester carbon, provide habitat for pollinators, and regulate our climate; they can also provide food, shelter, and a sense of well-being for humans. Simply put, all the benefits of an edible ecosystem can occur within a single micro-landscape (a 5' by 5' piece of yard, say) and can greatly influence the landscapes around it! This is a focus of *The Edible Ecosystem Solution:* that the micro-ecosystem can benefit the macro-landscape, that many small spots make global differences, and that the individual has the power for actual change today!

A micro-landscape installation next to a bandshell in the waterfront park in Cornwall, Ontario, in 2018.

Nearby to the installation shown above, the next logical step would be planting an edible hedge between the spot-planted hardwood trees along the extensive waterfront trails. The first planting is also a point of encouragement, education, and even plant material to help further ecosystem landscaping efforts.

Ecosystem Spot

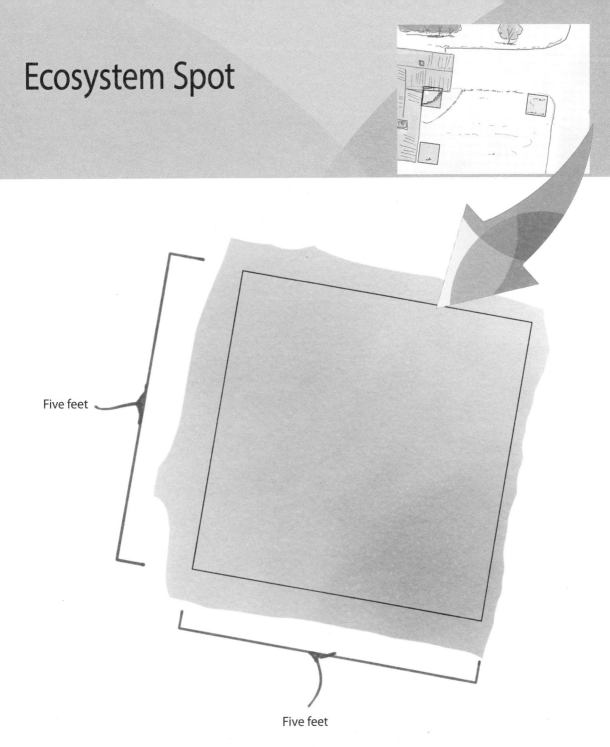

Five feet

Five feet

Finally, we zoom into a practical piece of land, the unit of possible achievement, and an effective goal for human habitat generation. What is the value of 25 square feet of lawn? Imagine the return on a spot of edible ecosystem compared to a typical micro-landscape of sod, or compacted dirt, or excess concrete!

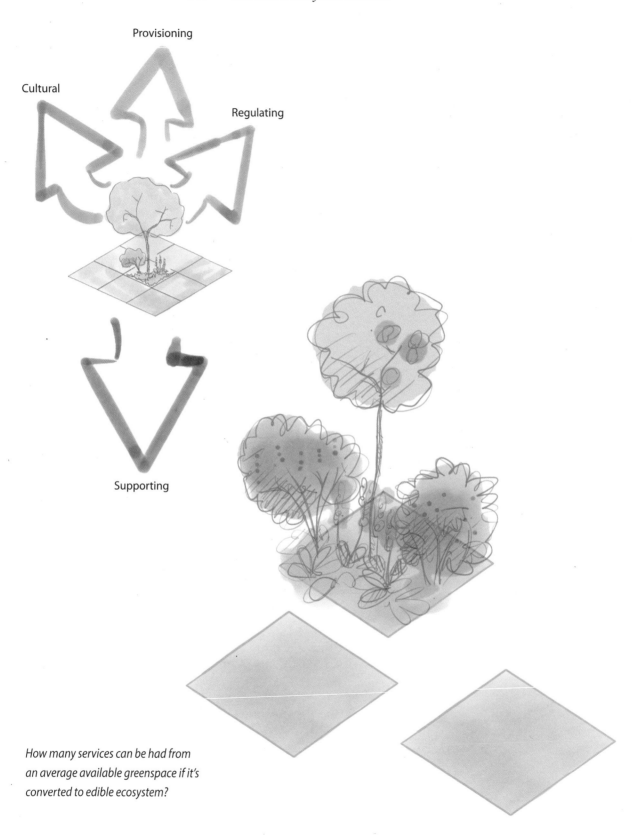

Provisioning

Cultural

Regulating

Supporting

How many services can be had from an average available greenspace if it's converted to edible ecosystem?

Value of 25 Square Feet

Speaking of human benefit from land, the value of any square footage of yard should be examined in terms of its input and output. What does it cost to care for an existing 25 square feet of lawn vs. the beneficial outputs of an edible ecosystem? We must consider the full services and potential and impact of our landscapes; every micro-landscape is worth investing in for higher return and less environmental degradation.

"The price of anything is the amount of life you exchange for it."

— Henry David Thoreau [22]

What is the cost/return of 25 square feet of edible ecosystem vs. lawn? Perhaps it is time to tip the scale in favor of land transition to edible diverse abundance!

Value of Lawn

The concept of the lawn was brought over from Europe; it has been a big part of the American Dream, and today lawns are found all over the world. However, this aesthetic goes against nature and requires great cost in space, time, energy, and money; lawns have even broader impacts when we consider pesticide pollution and water runoff, which causes further degradation to the environment. A recent study done in collaboration with NASA shows that there is currently three times more lawn in the United States than any other single crop, covering around 163,812 km2.[23]

Doing the math shows that Americans pay over $40 billion a year on lawns and large turfed areas.[24] This is a pretty penny to pay for landscapes that have *few direct benefits* and much *higher impacts* than alternatives such as edible landscapes, gardens, and wild ecosystems. The true cost of lawns should account for their considerable ecological footprint and the **opportunity cost** of what we have lost by not investing in more beneficial alternatives. Yes, it will cost more upfront to create biodiverse landscapes, but the long-term value is much higher, much like the investment in fuel-efficient vehicles vs. traditional gas-guzzlers. It's time to trade in so much lawn for something so much better.

Three Characteristics of Lawn

The aesthetic of the lawn has become a cultural standard (and obsession, with some folks) with three characteristics that have no grounding in natural science:

1. Most greenspaces/yards should be primarily just grass.

2. Lawns should be only a few chosen lawn species.

3. Grass must be regularly mowed to less than two inches.

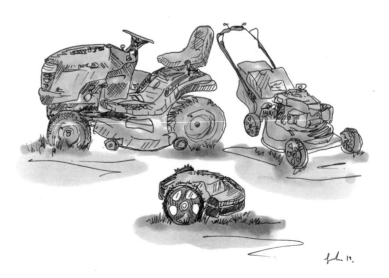

Many homeowners spend $1,000 to $20,000 on mowing equipment to support a low-service landscape.

Fighting Natural Succession

Attempting to keep our lawns as only grass is fighting natural succession, the tendency to more biodiverse systems, as well as the ability of ecosystems to self-regulate for water, fertility, and pests. Pure stands of a single species (monoculture) are rare in nature, and historically they never amounted to the vast acreages of sod we find today. The "weeds" in our lawns are there because there is an ecological niche to be filled—a bare patch of soil between grasses where sunlight, water, and nutrients are available, and more suitable to other species of plants. Natural systems want to find a balance, and in this, monocultures are essentially a red flag beckoning other species to come join the *underutilized* space. In addition, compacted, over-fertilized or under-fertilized soils will result in new species coming in to take advantage of conditions they particularly like. In fact, the excessive mowing of lawns only encourages weeds by giving them access to light. It is an uphill battle to have just grass. *Landscapes are diverse by nature.*

Herbicides, Pesticides, and Fertilizers

It is becoming widely known that herbicides kill bees and other pollinator species. In the US alone, some million pounds of pesticides are applied annually to lawns to control insects, weeds, and fungus. We should consider this in our treatment of that infamous "saboteur" of the perfect lawn aesthetic—the dandelion, a choice early spring treat for bees before they go about their busy jobs of pollinating flowers, orchards, and crops.

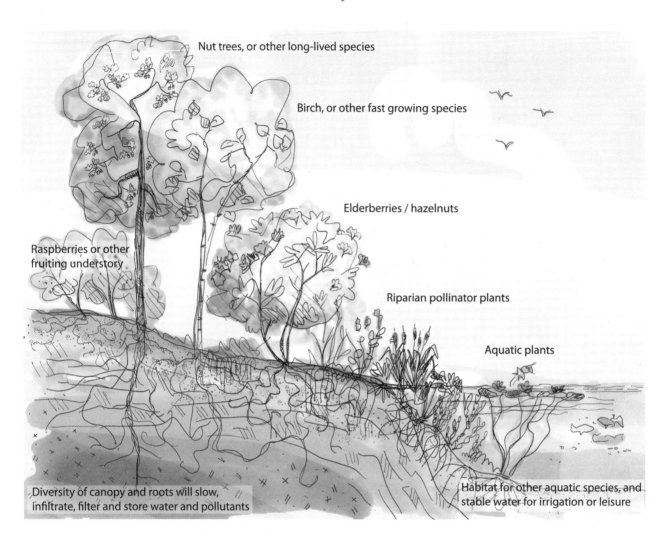

Nut trees, or other long-lived species

Birch, or other fast growing species

Elderberries / hazelnuts

Raspberries or other fruiting understory

Riparian pollinator plants

Aquatic plants

Diversity of canopy and roots will slow, infiltrate, filter and store water and pollutants

Habitat for other aquatic species, and stable water for irrigation or leisure

Watersheds around the world are polluted by pesticides, siltation, and waste; these could all be mitigated by greenspace transition to ecosystem land management. Riparian buffers are good examples; these can be integrated along municipal ditches and farmland watercourses to capture and use excess nutrient runoff. The EPA estimates that $1 spent on protecting the source of our freshwater provides $27 of water treatment savings.

The United States government could lead the way in Chesapeake restoration by demonstrating diversified land use throughout Washington DC's many public and national parks.

Losing Ecosystem Potential

Our lawn-scape is losing its ecosystem potential. The land is being degraded by compaction, low organic matter regeneration, and pollutant buildup. This is limiting soil life habitat and making the soil less able to provide services now and in the future. Healthy landscapes need diverse, layered ecosystems to be more productive, and this diversity ensures long-term potential for productivity. Many of our urban soils are severely damaged, and our agricultural soils are being eroded into lakes, rivers, and oceans. Movement away from monocultures (lawns or crops) is a return to soil security—which is quite literally the ground that supports all food and life.

Here, in South Africa, greenspace is being kept green at a high cost. Water loss to evaporation and runoff could be mitigated through a more pronounced urban tree canopy with diverse layers of foliage and roots for slowing, sinking, and storing water. Such management could yield higher returns, such as local food and wild spaces for community recreation.

Striking the Balance

Lawns *do* provide a certain aesthetic, recreational spaces, and a sense of comfort and security. As such, we need not convert every bit of lawn to edible landscapes—but let's prioritize *some* micro-landscapes to be transitioned to edible ecosystems, and their increased benefits (which *also include* typical yard services: aesthetics, reaction and a sense of comfort and security).

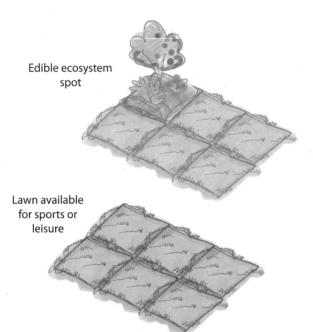

Edible ecosystem spot

Lawn available for sports or leisure

Left: *If you imagine your lawn divided into equal grids, you can fill in this monoculture graph paper with grass or edible diversity. We need not plant all our available lawn space as edible ecosystem, so long as we maximize some of the underutilized places in our communities.*

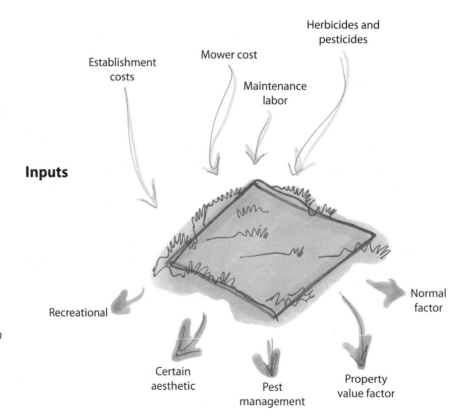

Inputs

Establishment costs

Mower cost

Maintenance labor

Herbicides and pesticides

Recreational

Certain aesthetic

Pest management

Property value factor

Normal factor

The input to lawns and the degradation they cause don't justify the returns and perceived benefits, many of which are less worthwhile when set beside edible ecosystem values.

The Value of Yard Ecosystems

The goods and services of edible ecosystems far outstrip that of lawn in direct and indirect benefit to humanity. The input vs. output—or expense vs. gain—for an edible micro-landscape is favorable enough to make it a good investment for any home. To convert a single 25-square-foot piece of lawn, there would be higher upfront cost in plants, but lower long-term costs in terms of fertilization, water, and mowing. If people stopped to think about it—and knew the realities of the true cost to the environment—they might change their thinking about lawns. They might decide it's time to put aesthetics and recreation aside because, arguably, ecosystems are hands-down more beautiful and recreational.

Conversion of lawn to ecosystem would make a big difference in what these areas produce relative to our investment and how they reduce our ecological footprint. Lawns transitioned to edible landscapes have more direct return from fewer inputs. A single mature fruit tree with herb companions can yield 300 pounds of fruit, produce 3,000 seeds, provide shade, reduce localized flooding, and provide habitat for birds, bees, and butterflies, and much more. All this in one 25-square-foot spot which otherwise would exist as costly compacted soil with a bit of drought-prone turf!

This small lawn yard on Long Island, New York, is barely big enough for leisure, and its cost of maintenance is high relative to its size and ecosystem benefits. It could, however, support a mature fruit tree that could yield hundreds of pounds of fruit with herbs for tea and cut flowers for the table.

This diverse raspberry planting in a micro-landscape yields nutrient-rich berries, and a pollinator garden provides habitat for bees and butterflies; both require minimal management, and both are great for small spaces.

Pollution or Solution?

Pollution and the loss of ecosystem opportunity have many causes from many acres, yards, and owners. The solution is transitioning to biodiversity and ecosystem services. This requires that homeowners opt in. From agriculture to public greenspace and yards, many owners must make the choice to diversify their landscapes. When it comes to lawns, this will require transforming the way we approach aesthetics, our personal values, and how property is valued. It will also require a cultural shift to influence varied stakeholders to transition whole landscapes bit by bit. Indeed, this is the argument at the crux of this book—multiple stakeholders can transition whole landscapes bit by bit; in so doing, they can catalyze a societal transformation. The next three sections of this book will present the how-to's of transitioning land affordably and effectively for real and lasting change. *Every bit of lawn has the potential to be a solution.*

What is the value of an old-growth tree? If we allow our ecosystems to grow, they provide immense services. Imagine old-growth food forests in our communities…oh, yes!

Section 3

Edible Ecosystem Design

ANY BIT OF YARD CAN BECOME A BEAUTIFUL, EDIBLE PIECE OF EDEN—just outside your front door. When we focus on small and achievable goals, we often get superb results. Any 25-square-foot piece of lawn can be a site for ecosystem design and transitioned using an easy step-by-step process into a diverse, abundant, and beautiful edible micro-landscape. An edible ecosystem is more than just a delicious and enjoyable part of your landscape. It can start an affordable and effective transition of your yard to a truly wonderful human habitat. This section will dive into edible ecosystem design: including site selection, *Permabed* construction, and food guild layout and planting. It includes the first five steps of the *EPI System** (the remaining steps are given in Section 4). Together, Sections 3 and 4 form the backbone of ***The Edible Ecosystem Solution.*** They present a path forward for actual, actionable change today!

* The EPI System, described in Section 4, is a design framework for transitioning communities to edible biodiversity and community resilience.

Inspiration to Act

Imagine children climbing a mature apricot tree in your front yard, eating the fresh fruit and spitting the pits into the soil below, knowing the next generation can grow there in the mother's shade. Imagine picking fresh strawberries, raspberries, and currants and juicing them into smoothies or cocktails for a weekend get-together. Think of how enjoyable it would be to pick bunches of mint for lemonade to beat the heat in the summertime.

Modern Edible Ecosystem

Any spot can be turned into a small garden bed and planted with a mix of edible food plants. We layer these plants for companionships by mimicking natural form and function. What follows is a step-by-step process for transitioning any 5' by 5' piece of ground—by anyone, anywhere—to become something new: a bit of a modern, edible ecosystem. We are creating a micro-landscape that is really a piece of human habitat, similar to what our ancestors enjoyed and what our minds, bodies, and souls so intrinsically crave.

This one bit of yard you are transitioning can provide so much joy to family, friends, and the community: birds might sing in branches, butterflies may flutter around herbs, and there could be a shady spot for a hammock chair. To have this in one's yard is gratifying; to have it in every yard would be a wonder for society. Both are very achievable with soil turning, plant selection, and ecosystem design.

Your Spot, Any Spot

Remember, your edible landscape can be anywhere. It could be any little corner of yard, community garden, neighborhood park, or even a city tree well. Working with your family, neighbors, municipal councils, and other organizations, we can maximize the many bits of underutilized community land to become ecosystem spots. If it is a discernible micro-landscape, it can yield diverse, edible abundance.

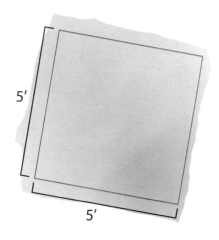

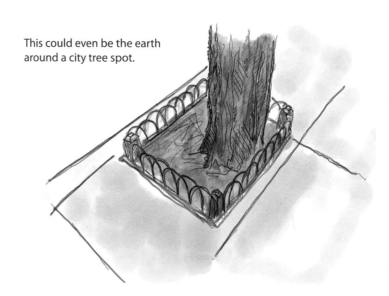

This could even be the earth around a city tree spot.

This tree well in New York seems to be begging for a diverse understory. Look into your local bylaws concerning planting and care of city trees, many municipalities would be open, if not eager to have citizens take ownership of the care and longevity of street trees and the beautification of urban neighborhoods.

Every piece of land has the capacity to support a unique mixture of plants. Any 5' x 5' site is a good candidate for a food plant guild! A site that already has a tree at its center can have companion herbs and berries placed in the four corners, and groundcover can grow around it all.

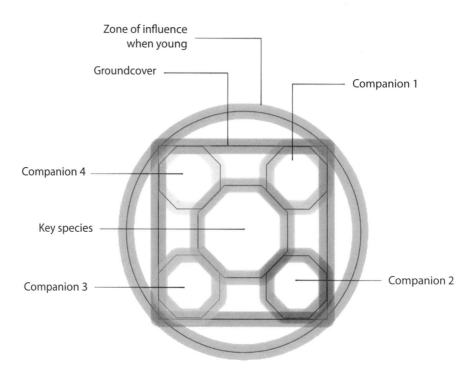

Zone of influence when young

Groundcover

Companion 1

Companion 4

Key species

Companion 3

Companion 2

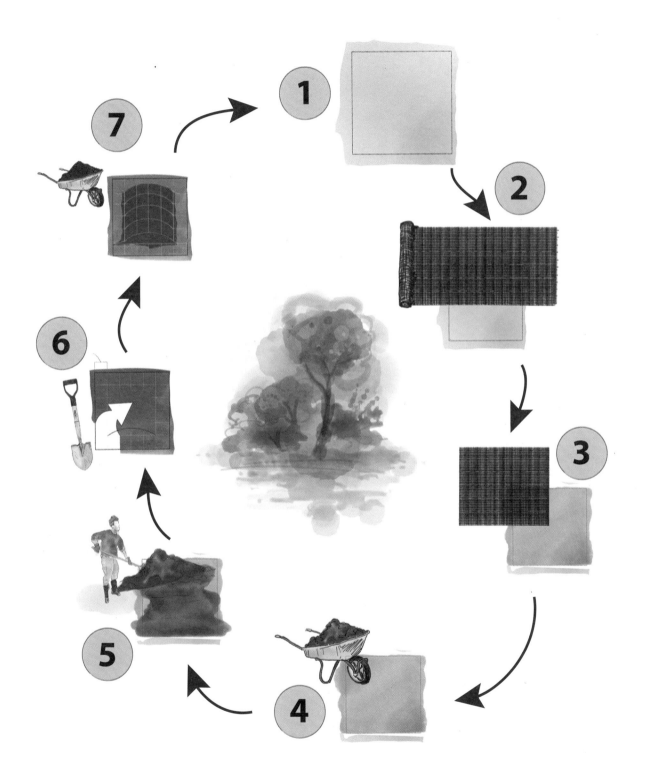

Let's first look at how we can go from a grass spot (1) to a raised bed (7) affordably and effectively; then, we'll consider what and how to plant to make it into an edible ecosystem.

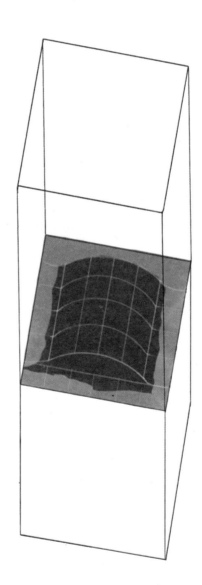

Now, let's zoom into our spot of Earth *and see what lies within this micro-environment. Understanding your future garden's environment is crucial to edible ecosystem design for biodiversity benefits.*

Unique Environment

Your garden has its own unique environment below, above, and around your garden bed. Just like the environment of our planet, a garden site's micro-environment can be visualized as a 5' by 5' square column that rises into the air 10' and goes into the ground 10'; this column is primarily composed of air, water, and minerals. Each landscape spot has atmosphere, lithosphere, and hydrosphere that we should understand in order to choose the best plants for our soil and climate, as well as considering the space available for a future edible ecosystem to grow above and below ground.

Below Ground

Let's look deeper at the structure of the soil in a single 5' x 5' column. Roots can penetrate quite deep into the soil if there is good soil structure. Consider the deep-rooted prairie plants or the root structures of trees—they need space to grow. Soil structure includes the arrangement of soil **aggregates**—the building blocks of soil—and these form the basis of habitat for microorganisms as part of a functioning **soil food web** benefiting your future plants.

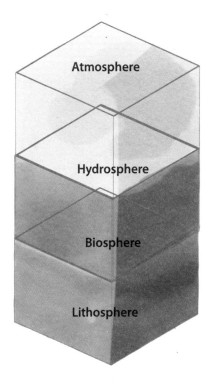

Plants are very dynamic and in constant interaction with their environment. Finding plants that are suitable to your site's specific environment will ensure success.

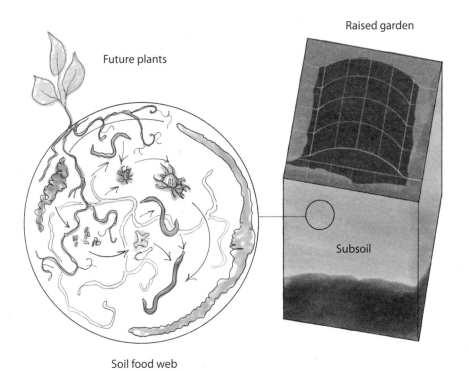

Future plants

Raised garden

Subsoil

Soil food web

Soil organisms make homes in aggregates that hold air, water, and organic matter; the aggregates are made of clay, sand, and silt grains stuck together by organic matter, roots, and clay adhesion.

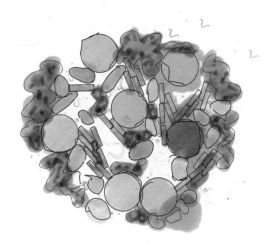

Soil aggregates—the home of soil life and the basis of productive soil—are made of different mineral particles: sand, silt, clay, as well as organic matter, air, and water.

Soil Sampling Is Easy

The nutrients, organic matter content, mineral texture, and other information in your soil can be determined at a cost of about $40 by taking a soil sample and sending it to a lab. Make sure to get the instructions from the lab you choose about how to take a soil sample. It's not hard to determine a soil's texture on your own. Texture is the measure of sand, silt, and clay particle size and their relative composition within a sample of soil. Sand gives better drainage, whereas clay has better nutrient and water retention. An overall good soil is called *loam* (a mix of sand, silt, and clay). If you squeeze a handful of soil and it forms a squished shape, it has mostly clay; if it crumbles like cake, it is well-mixed loam; if the grains fall from between your fingers, it is mostly sand.

The Above-Ground Environment

Now let's consider the space above your garden site. First, we need to know where the sun shines and how much light hits the ground of your site. Then we'll examine how much room there is for a tree to grow and consider how much light would reach the food plants when we plant a guild.

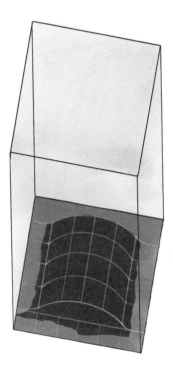

Consider the above-ground space available for your ecosystem to grow

Your micro-landscape has space available for growth and an overall exposure of full or partial sun, or even full shade. This above-ground environment needs some scrutiny in order to choose site-suitable plants.

Your garden spot has a sunny-side

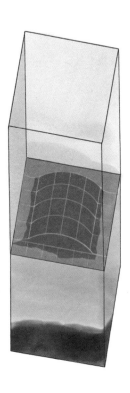

Finding the Sun

Your garden has four sides relative to the sun. Which side is south? This information helps organize sun-loving plants. At noon, take two garden stakes and a string, tie the string to both stakes, and stick stake #1 in the ground near your bed. Now line up the string's shadow with the shadow of stake #1 by adjusting stake #2 before you stick it into the ground. Your string is running parallel to the shadow cast from the north side of stake #1. If you draw an arrow in the soil, it will point to solar south. Sun-loving plants will thrive on this side of your future edible ecosystem.

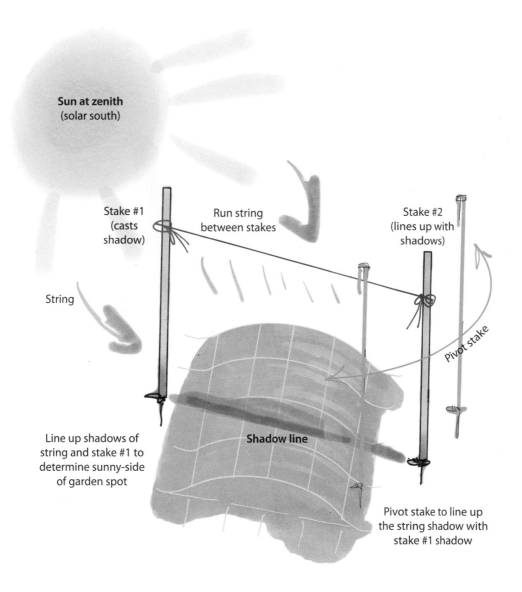

Sun at zenith
(solar south)

Stake #1
(casts
shadow)

Run string
between stakes

Stake #2
(lines up with
shadows)

String

Pivot stake

Line up shadows of
string and stake #1 to
determine sunny-side
of garden spot

Shadow line

Pivot stake to line up
the string shadow with
stake #1 shadow

Finding Shade

Now, you would benefit by knowing how much shade your overall site receives throughout the season. You figure this out by observing the shadows that nearby objects (trees, buildings, fences) cast on your spot in the spring and summer. How often is your spot in full shade, full sun, or partial shade? Many yards have shady nooks, which, although they are not ideal for huge fruit trees, can be maximized with shade-tolerant food plants.

*These **Planting Points**, designated by yellow, red, and blue dots, are colored based on sun and shade for the placement of garden plants.*

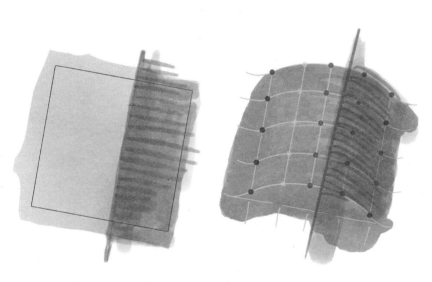

Full sun micro-landscapes are the best for fruit; partial-shade sites can still yield good berries, and full shade is great for summer herbs, salad greens, and specialty woodland medicinal plants. Mint is an option for partial-shade and to fill in an area completely with aromatic and beautiful foliage. Creeping thymes are less aggressive for areas where you don't want your garden spot to spread too much and a good groundcover is needed.

The best way to find shade is to study your site three times per day. Go outside in the morning, afternoon, and evening and observe where the shadows fall (or don't fall). Was your site fully shaded at 7 AM, no shade at noon, and no shade at 5 PM? If so, this is a sunny spot with good afternoon sun. If it was half-shaded all three times, this is a partially shaded spot. If it was shaded all day, then this is a full-shade spot. If you do this on the first day of each month from April to September (or November to April in Southern Hemisphere), you will get a good sense of the sun/shade for the whole growing season. Get a garden notebook and set an alarm. It only takes a few minutes per month.

Room to Grow

Everything needs room to grow. This garden design is 5' long and 5' wide. We now understand its soil depth, but how much room around and above your bed exists for a squash to sprawl, a raspberry to bush out, and a tree to spread up and out? This can easily be eyeballed or measured. How far from every corner of your garden to the next object? How much room is needed for access? Can you pass with a wheelbarrow on at least one side?

Remember, there is no *bad spot* for a garden bed, but there is a right plant for the chosen spot. If you look up and you have telephone wires overhead, don't plant a big tree! If your site is cornered between the wing of the house and the garage, don't plant a medium tree that will overwhelm the building. If your spot is along the walkway up to the house, don't plant something so bushy that it will crowd the walkway.

Large trees, like this oak, need much more room than a dwarf cherry, and this should be considered when analyzing your site.

Build a Permabed

Now, let's focus on the surface of our micro-landscape and build up our potential for ecosystem services. Building a garden bed is pretty straightforward—when you know what to do from the get-go.

Bye-bye Grass

First things first: most **potential sites** have either grass or a mix of weeds in a failing lawn. If you have bare soil, then skip ahead, but otherwise, we need to remove these "weeds" to start establishing our desired ecology. A low-cost and passive way of doing this is to cover the site with a piece of weed barrier or black poly tarp.* Buy a 6'-wide roll and cut a 6' piece to cover your **site**. Weigh down the weed barrier with anything heavy along the entire edge to keep the wind from carrying it away. One option is to use small straw bales or long piles of wood chips along the edge. (Later, these organic materials make excellent mulch.)

Now, if we leave the weed barrier down for an entire growing season (April to October), it will kill plants growing underneath—frying the grass and weed seeds. In addition, the covering makes sure most of the nitrogen and other nutrients go into the soil instead of the atmosphere. Depending on your weed pressure and ambient temperatures, the process may only require two to three months.

* Weed barrier can be purchased in rolls of various widths and lengths at most garden supply stores. The highest-quality weed barrier comes from greenhouse supply stores. Consider asking local farmers at farmers markets where to find good supplies.

Weed barrier can be used before planting. Consider asking local farmers at farmers markets where to find good supplies. Community knowledge-sharing is an important resource to exchange between the countryside and cities.

Transition Aesthetics

Transition aesthetics are important. This is your yard, and it's in the public eye—we want to impress with the beauty and possibility of our yards to be human habitat, right? So, if you can cover the whole weed barrier with wood chips (so it isn't too unsightly) and plant something to grow over the barrier as it kills the grass without the use of chemicals—all the better!

Cut a small hole in the center of the weed barrier, dig a deep hole, and plant zucchini or pumpkin, so something beautiful is growing in the meantime. Squashes are an easy starter crop (use healthy transplants for better growth in colder regions) and can be quite fun for children! You could also select some annual flowers and plant through holes in the barrier to fill in the area and attract pollinators.

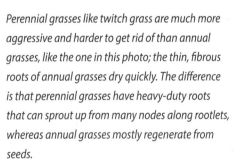

Perennial grasses like twitch grass are much more aggressive and harder to get rid of than annual grasses, like the one in this photo; the thin, fibrous roots of annual grasses dry quickly. The difference is that perennial grasses have heavy-duty roots that can sprout up from many nodes along rootlets, whereas annual grasses mostly regenerate from seeds.

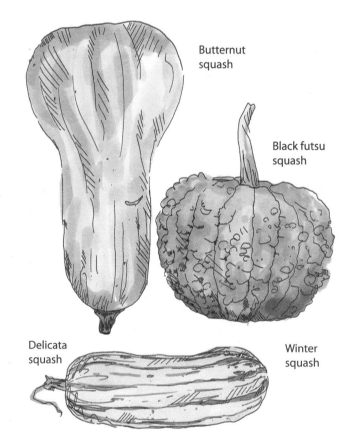

Butternut squash

Black futsu squash

Delicata squash

Winter squash

How to Build Quality Soil

1. Get a soil test.
2. Balance major *soil components* through amendments.
3. Add quality compost with balanced nitrogen, carbon, and major nutrients.
4. Test for micronutrients and adjust your soil.
5. Introduce beneficial soil life through compost teas and specific inoculants.
6. Reduce compaction with raised beds and organic matter.
7. Improve soil with biodiverse plantings.
8. Protect soil life over winter with cover crops and perennials.
9. Remember to select site-suitable plants—you can only change your soil so much!

Once the weeds are removed, it is time to improve your soil. It is helpful to improve soil at the get-go to give your future edible ecosystem a boost. This includes understanding holistic soil principles and how to build quality soil.

Soil aggregates are the houses and apartment buildings for soil life. Yes, your soil is alive! Adding compost and reducing compaction is critical to soil life.

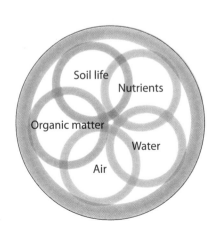

Soil life
Nutrients
Organic matter
Water
Air

"Holistic soil" is a term we can use to describe a living, functioning soil in which all major components are interconnected and function as a whole—giving and receiving ecosystem goods and services.

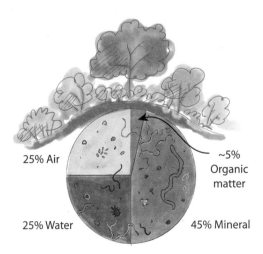

25% Air

~5% Organic matter

25% Water

45% Mineral

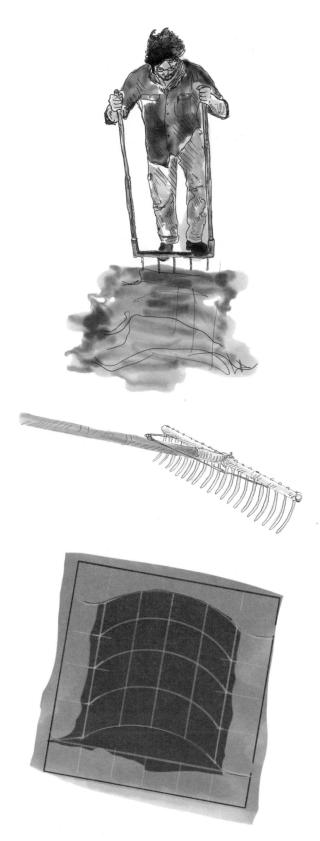

Turning over a New Bed

Now that we have an understanding of preparing a site for holistic soil, it's time to form a *Permabed* (a raised garden bed) to improve your site further. Get a thermos of lemonade with fresh mint and head outside with a sturdy shovel. (A great shovel should have little turned metal footpads and an ergonomic handle.)

Now is the time to *double dig* the whole 5' by 5' area with your shovel. Double digging means you shovel in, and turn soil and compost, and then shovel deeper into the now loosened soil, and turn it again. You are effectively mixing and loosening the local soil with the compost mix, similar to a rototiller or a plow on a commercial farm. However, in the case of a garden spot, you will never need to dig this much or deep, again. You can also use a **broad fork** (a very sturdy digging fork with extra-long tines). In the future, if you want to loosen the garden bed, this is the only tool needed; it acts as a subsoiler.

Okay, now dig a 1'-wide and 6"-deep flat trench on the perimeter of your **chosen site** and put the excavated soil into the middle area to create a raised mound over top of the loosened soil. This area should end up at least 12" above the original grade of the site. Now, the garden bed can be raked into a smooth bed top. You can cross-rake from one side to the other and then from the opposite ends again to make an even, slightly convex mound. The bigger soil clods of soil can be broken apart with the rake, and also pulled into the path (where they will be broken down by foot traffic). The best rakes are wide, around 36", with long tines, and a long handle that is ergonomic when used standing fully erect (no hunched raking, please!).

Work back and forth along the length of your 5' bed to create a smooth and slightly convex shape. The shoulders of the bed can gradually meet the flat ground at a 35° angle. It doesn't have to be perfect; just have another drink of lemonade, and tidy it up till it looks good to you!

Permabed Architecture

Your new garden spot is essentially a micro raised garden bed. This can be referred to as a **Permabed**, because, unlike garden areas that are tilled flat every years, this garden spot is permanent. If used for vegetables, you may choose to reform it and loosen it again with a broad fork, but it will never change location.

The *Permabed* has four key features: a bed top, shoulder, path, and core. The bed top is for planting, watering, and weeding. The path is for cover crop and/or chip mulch for accessibility. The shoulder are meant to help maintain and stabilize the bed top, periodically weeded or mulched as needed. The core is for the soil life to develop a healthy ecosystem and build symbiotic relationships with your food plant guilds.

Permabeds can be any size. These dimensions are ideal for many micro-landscapes.

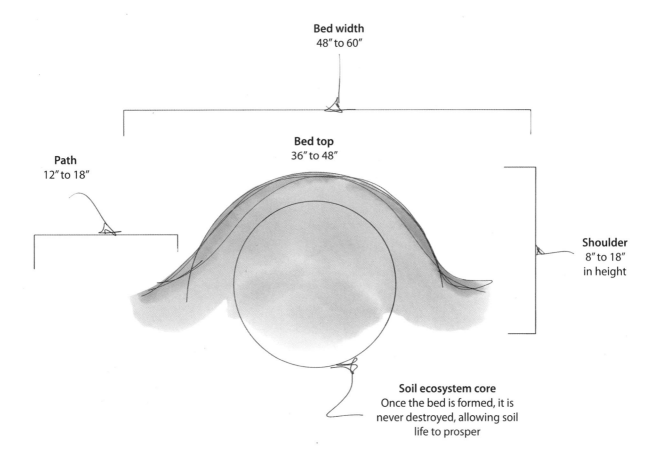

Bed width
48" to 60"

Bed top
36" to 48"

Path
12" to 18"

Shoulder
8" to 18"
in height

Soil ecosystem core
Once the bed is formed, it is never destroyed, allowing soil life to prosper

Layered form

Microclimate regulation

Pollinator habitat

Nutrient sharing

Soil building

Ecosystem Mimicry for a Functional Landscape*

An ecosystem must be able to function properly to provide services. As micro-landscape designers, we need to mimic natural ecosystem form and function in order to achieve a landscape's true potential. All ecosystems have plants of different shapes and sizes, and they all function differently for the benefit of the larger ecosystem. We can design ecosystem form and function into our micro-landscapes by emulating the diverse layers we see in natural ecosystems.

* For more information on ecosystem mimicry please visit www.ecosystemsolutioninstitute.com.

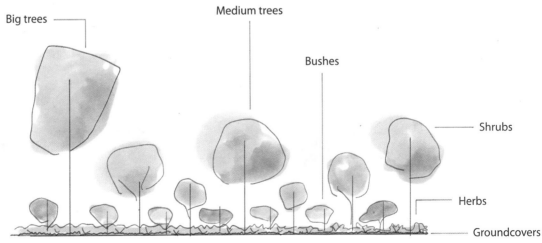

Big trees

Medium trees

Bushes

Shrubs

Herbs

Groundcovers

Edible Ecosystem Layers

Ecosystems have layers: a woodland has big trees, medium ones, smaller shrubs, bushes, groundcovers of herbs, and creeping plants. Gardens should be layered like an ecosystem for maximum use of incoming solar energy and diversifying the form of leaves, shoots, and roots within a limited piece of ground.

Different plants require more or less space above and around them to grow. Larger trees will alter the sun's access to the rest of the yard when they are fully grown. Although we will be primarily discussing woodland ecosystem layering, it is important to remember all ecosystems need layering—prairies and riparian buffers included. We will also look at these layers through the lens of both their use for humans and their benefits for each other as companionship species. We want to make sure to include a mix of plant sizes, but also of functions, such as fruit production, nitrogen-fixation, soil protection, and pollinator habitat.

1. **Big Tree:** This layer is composed of larger trees, including edible mangoes (subtropics), maples (mid-latitudes), or Korean nut pines (cold climates). Remember, it will take many years for this tree to become full-grown, and if you already have a well-loved shade tree, consider planting a replacement now because all trees eventually senesce,* and some can be lost in storms or from disease.

2. **Medium Tree:** This layer includes many popular fruit trees on their natural rootstocks, such as apples, pears, and plums. Medium trees usually reach a maximum height of about 25 to 40 feet.

3. **Shrub:** This includes many smaller trees that usually have multiple stems and grow between ten and sixteen feet tall such as hazelnuts, elderberries, and sour cherries.

4. **Bush:** This includes popular raspberries, shade-tolerant currants, and haskap (a cold-hardy favorite). Berry and other bushes tend to grow to a maximum height of about three to four feet. They are easy to propagate yourself.

5. **Vine/Epiphytes:** Vines include grapes and hardy kiwi; epiphytes can include orchids, etc.

6. **Groundcover:** These include low-growing plants such as thyme, moss, lichens, some clovers, etc. These are critical for stabilizing soil and reducing erosion.

* Senescence is the slow eventual death and decay of trees; it may take 75 to 5,000 years.

7. **Herb:** Herbs fit nicely between the other larger food plants and patterned nicely in your micro-landscape (see Garden Patterning). Many herbs grow between 6 and 24 inches off the ground; examples are chives, lemon balm, and violets. Many pest confuser plants are in this layer.

8. **Annuals/Biennials:** These include all the vegetables and some herbs in cold climates. Many important pollinator habitat plants are included here.

9. **Fungi:** Includes edible mushrooms like shiitake, chanterelle, and medicinals, like reishi and chaga.

10. **Soil:** This is its own layer, and a microcosm on its own—full of beneficial soil organisms.

11. **Riparian/Aquatic:** This includes plants that grow best either fully or partially in water; examples include cattails, marsh marigold, and lotus.

12. **Animal:** This is a large food web of its own to consider; it might contain chickens, goats, frogs, and more.

Thyme is wonderful groundcover and confuses pests of fruit trees due to its high concentration of aromatic oils. Violets are a great shade-loving groundcover, and they make a wonderful liquor for cocktails. In France, Toulouse is famous for its violet treats.

Plant Selection for Regional Hardiness

There are many plant options for your garden. Now that we know the layers we want to mimic and some of the important functions and services plants can perform, we should consider which will survive in our area. Of primary importance is finding plants that will be suitable for your regional climate. Plant hardiness is a measure of plant survival at average winter low temperatures. If your plant cannot survive your winter lows, it will not be worth planting.

Fruit trees can create a true legacy on a property. This cherry tree was planted in a yard in the 1990s and now yields copious cherries. Now that the family that planted it has moved, the cherry tree gives fresh fruit to a new family. Alongside the traditional Ukrainian birdhouse, this tree serves as a beautiful sight for the family when they visit the neighborhood and reminisce.

Site-suitable plants are those that not only provide delicious and useful treats; they have to be able to survive in your area.

Suitable to Micro-Environment

The food plants you choose must be site-suitable to your landscape's environment. This means finding plants that will grow well in your soil, shade/sun exposure, and other environmental circumstances. From our discussion on environment, it should be clear that although we can improve fertility and drainage for a garden, the overall pH and sun/shade of a given spot must be respected when choosing plants. In an urban environment, it is also important to consider abrasive forces such as bikes, the effect of salts applied for de-icing roads, and extreme summer heat from anthropogenic sources adding to normal temperature swings.

Local and Traditional Knowledge

The value of neighbors, local nurseries, and traditional knowledge in choosing plants for your garden shouldn't be underestimated. Indeed, they are probably the best sources for suggestions for successful plant choices. Ask for suggestions from avid gardeners, join a garden club, and find local nurseries that grow their own tree stock. Imported trees that are only displayed in a nursery provide little information on how well they do in your area. Traditional Environmental Knowledge (TEK) includes insight into heirloom varieties, site-suitable plants, and guild design.

Food plants should be first selected for regional hardiness and then for the microclimate of your landscape.

These ripening saskatoon (aka juneberries) will be a wonderful summer treat. Saskatoons are a traditional food of the prairie and woodland edge ecosystem of North America. They are cold hardy, disease-resistant, and highly nutritious.

Design an
Ecosystem Guild

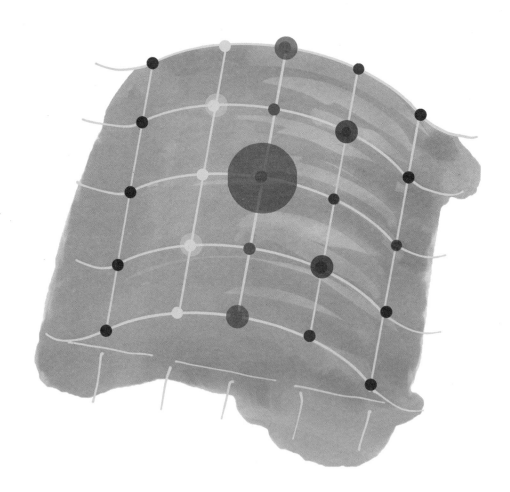

Now, let's focus on your spot's future *by creating a design that mimics ecosystem form, function, and potential.*

Guild Design Process

Guild design is a process of creating a good layout, assessing site-suitable food plants, and selecting appropriate key and companion varieties. It is also about understanding how to pattern the form and function of your plants so they partition resources, are mutually beneficial, and contribute to overall ecosystem health.

A guild is a companionship of plants that work well together as a micro-ecosystem within the local environment. Annual guilds like corn, beans, and squash are traditional and popular. But perennial guilds offer more long-term services to society.

Permabed System for Biodiversity

The Permabed System is a form of edible ecosystem design organized for efficient management to maximize ecosystem services.

The Permabed System was developed for productive and efficient edible ecological landscape management for farmers, gardeners, and landscape designers. It is described fully for commercial farms in the book: *The Permaculture Market Garden.* The following pages will discuss this system in detail for *micro-landscape design* and then expanding on these principles for *macro-landscape*

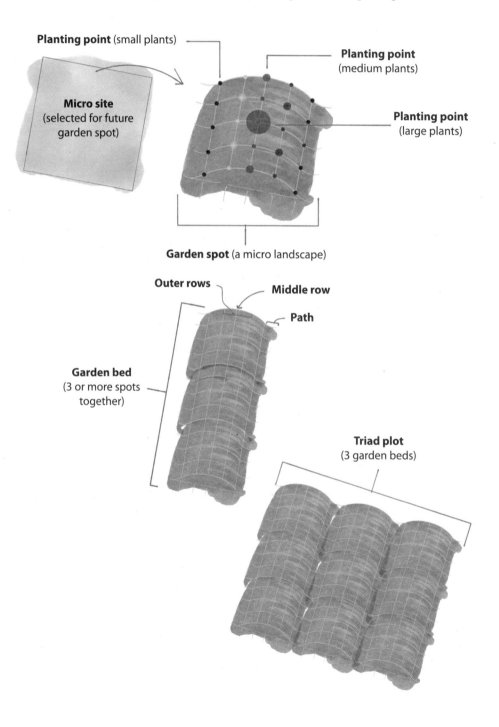

Planting point (small plants)

Planting point (medium plants)

Micro site (selected for future garden spot)

Planting point (large plants)

Garden spot (a micro landscape)

Outer rows

Middle row

Path

Garden bed (3 or more spots together)

Triad plot (3 garden beds)

design. There is key jargon to understand to communicate the effective design; these are in bold and found within the full-page infographics. In this system, any **Site** can be turned into an edible micro-landscape or edible ecosystem. The basic design elements for this system are **Planting Points, Guild Spots, Permabeds,** and **Triad Plots**.

Small planting point
(Blue = shade tolerant)

* For small plants, such as groundcovers

Medium planting point
(Yellow = sun-loving)

* For medium plants, such as herbs

Large planting point
(Red = key species, access to sun from height above other companions)

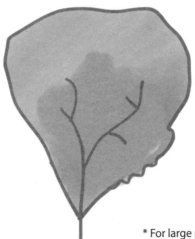

* For large plants, such as berry bushes, fruit trees, and in some cases large trees, such as nuts

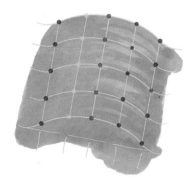

Layout and Organization

Layout is fundamental for organization, and organization is critical for the success of any diversified planting. As such, the *Permabed System* outlines how to lay out a garden spot for organized ecosystem plantings. First, vocabulary: a **planting point** is anywhere you dig a hole and place a plant; **a guild spot** is any 5' by 5' garden area; a **row** is any line of planting (often sunny or shady); a **bed** is any assembly of multiple garden spots in line together.

The Key Plant

Guilds are designed around a **key species** or food plant. This food plant anchors the guild like a ship at sea and forms the basis for management and design. Your key food plant might be chosen based on a mixture of reasons, including the goals you set for your garden. Essentially, what do you want to eat? You'll want to give this some thought because these key plants are often the largest and/or the longest-living plant in the guild. Goals, size, and longevity, should be considered in selecting your key species.

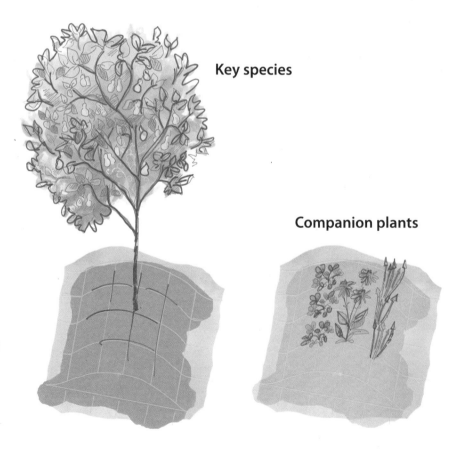

Key species

Companion plants

Here, a pear tree will be the key species; it is long-lived, large, and of high value to the steward of this particular guild garden. Companion plants are planned to accompany the key species. Pest deterrents, or confusers, will be planted to help with pest management, and groundcovers will protect the soil from erosion.

Companion Plants

Your guild needs companion plants for your key species. Companions are plants that work well with the key plant. They should, of course, benefit the guild as a whole, be of value to you, and perhaps have specific benefits for the key species, such as deterring its pests. A good rule of thumb is finding plants that make up different layers within an ecosystem. A full or partial complement of layers will balance well in a guild planting.

Garden Patterning

Garden patterns help you with garden design and assist in the final selection of exactly which plants and what quantities to select. This layout schematic shows variously sized **colored planting points.** Each point's size is relative to the size of the plant to be situated there (large, medium, or small). In this example design of a woodland ecosystem, the points are for a tree, herbs, and groundcover (another guild example will follow at the end of this chapter).

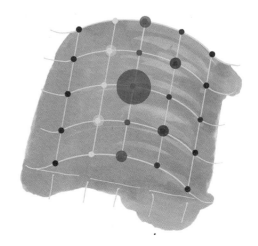

Every *planting point* between your rows and cross lines is a spot for planting. This layout shows that each section of the bed is also best planted in appropriate types of plants. The paths are best in groundcovers and/or mulched (green); the sunny side is best in sun-loving herbs or berries (yellow); the center row is best planted in larger food plants that will reach the sun by growing up (red); the shady side of the garden bed is best planted in shade-tolerant herbs and/or berries (blue).

Notice the largest point is at the center. This is for your **key plant** (the fruit tree here). Around the key plant, we alternate the size of the color points between groundcovers (small points) and herbs (medium). The path points are all the same size, indicating that they are most suitable to be planted with small, low-growing groundcover. The basic alternating of size provides a good balance of resource partitions and ensures diversity. For instance, medium spots could be planted with medicinal flowers, vegetables, nitrogen-fixing clover,* or a grapevine.

* Red clovers can be quite robust and are suitable for medium plant points; others, like dwarf white clover or alsike, can serve well as groundcovers.

Guild Pattern Considerations

- **Size of Plants:** The size of the plant at maturity is considered to make sure two large plants aren't planted too close to one another; also, the best resource partitioning occurs when dissimilar plants are adjacent rather than next to plants with identical leaf and root patterns.
- **Ecological Layer of Plants:** Plants of different layers companion well and provide diverse services.
- **Sun- or Shade-Loving/Tolerant:** Make sure that plants are suitable to the sun or shadiness of the area as a whole as well as planted in the appropriate row based on relative shadiness once the ecosystem grows in.
- **Function:** Find plants that serve different functions for the garden guild, such as nitrogen fixers, nectar sources for bees, and pest deterrents.

A proper guild design will have plants with alternating forms and functions. This way, your ecosystem has plants of different sizes that partition resources and plants that offer various services to you, the other plants, and the system as a whole.

Plant a Micro-Landscape

Let's zoom into ourselves and get the job done right—by planting
our design, our vision, our own piece of ecosystem.

Tidy Planting Rows

The best thing you can do before planting is to make some nice, tidy planting rows (preferably east to west), but most important is staying in-line with other common landscape lines. There are many ways to do this. The easiest way is to push some 6" tube cut-offs (from an old garden hose) onto your rake tines 8"–12" apart. Run the rake along the length of the bed for equidistant, defined rows. You can then cross-rake to produce squared markings on your bed top. Both of these can be used to help with food plant guild design.

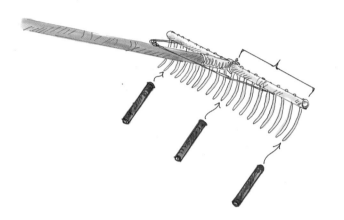
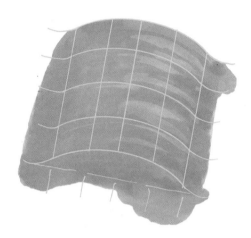

The Sunny Side of Life

Let's say you have marked three rows for planting on a garden bed. The rows are oriented east to west. This means one of the rows is on the sunny side. Let's call it the "Sunny Row." Sun-loving plants should be kept on the sunny side of your garden, and more shade-tolerant plants on the shady side. This is of particular importance for groundcovers and herbs. Note that your large tree or bushes will get more sun from the middle row because of their size and form.

Plant Your Guild

Now it is time to plant your guild properly. When you know your layout, dig a hole and place the plant in it, with its roots spread out, like a hand. Take care not to plant too deeply; you don't want to bury the plant stalk. Note where the roots start to appear on the stem and place the plant in the hole so that this spot is one inch above the level ground. Refill the hole with the soil and press down to firm the soil. The point where the roots start on the stalk should now be about half an inch below ground level.

Planting is easy, but make sure you don't use rootbound transplants, which are the result of plants being kept too long in a too-small pot. They will have many tightly packed roots growing in a circle around hard, compacted soil. We need to start to prioritize the use of bare-root saplings. The most expensive trees are those in pots, and they are the least healthy.

Mulching

Now is time for mulching the edges of the bed. You can apply sheet mulching of cardboard or weed barrier around your bed. On top of this layer, place three inches of woodchips. This creates a quality barrier against grass encroachment into your micro edible ecosystem. It also allows you to remove it when you need to, and it allows your edible ecosystem to spread as it matures.

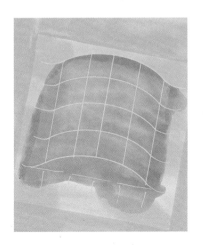

Chips provide a good border for your edible garden. This helps with access and prevents the encroachment of weeds and aggressive grasses. Most lawn sod isn't aggressive; of more concern are perennial grasses, which have very persistent roots.

Ecosystem Options

Remember our discussion of environment, climate, and the major planetary biomes—there are *ecosystem* and *edible ecosystem solutions* for all. As designers, we need a vision and goals to approach our landscape design process; we can choose to restore native vegetation or plant site-suitable edible and useful varieties.

For instance, we can plant woodland guilds with all native species such as chokecherry, pin cherry, and saskatoon. Or we might include a domestic pear variety alongside a wild saskatoon. Whether designing for a small patch of land, whole properties, or public spaces, this chapter will exemplify guilds for anyone, anywhere, and it will show how small garden spots can be expanded for macro-landscape installations.

It is important to remember that there are more temperate and tropical versions of all ecosystems. Temperature, precipitation, and the soil are big factors in selecting which ecosystems you'll want to work with.

Your Vision and Goals

Consider the overall goal when designing an ecosystem guild—is it food production, land restoration, pollinator habitat creation? For instance, the goal could be restoration of degraded landscapes, like those found in formerly over-grazed areas in New Mexico. The *hügelkultur* beds (seen here) use the Permabed System to organize effective *ecosystem restoration guilds*. These are installed on eroding micro-sites (near rivulets leading to a larger arroyo) to reduce soil loss, improve landscape integrity, and serve as sources of seed dispersal for macro-landscape regeneration of native species.

New planting site (once this spot is filled to a good height for a raised bed, built a new hugelkultur bed further up the landscape)

Small square strawbale

Local soil dam

Trapped silt and soil

Bury dead fall branches

Stones help water sink

This small site is designed to trap eroding soil and silt, slow and sink water, and become a productive growing bed for native vegetation restoration.

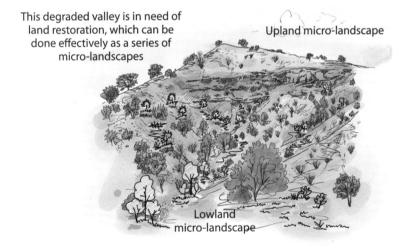

This degraded valley is in need of land restoration, which can be done effectively as a series of micro-landscapes

Upland micro-landscape

Lowland micro-landscape

Many of these small sites across a larger degraded landscape (such as the valley seen here), provide macro land regeneration.

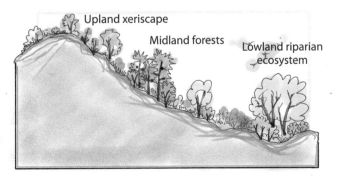

Upland xeriscape

Midland forests

Lowland riparian ecosystem

Northern New Mexico land restoration design for 6,000 to 7,000 feet elevation

Each micro-landscape can be designed with different site-suitable guilds of appropriate plants for native ecosystems, such as those found in the lowland, midslopes, and uplands in a region (such as this ecosystem profile of northern New Mexico). These sites also serve as seed sources for animal and wind dispersal of important native species regeneration.

Fruit Woodland: Goal = High Food Production

This fruit micro-landscape mimics the form and function of a deciduous woodland ecosystem. Rather than a more random complement of plant species found in a wild woodland, this garden spot has a selection of chosen edible and useful plants following a specific ecosystem design. Fruit woodlands center on small, medium, or large-sized trees, depending on your site and goals. Possible candidates for key species are nut, fruit, or other productive trees. Note, if you already have a large tree in your yard, then you have a candidate for a garden spot with mostly small trees or bushes to fill in an edible understory. Or, if you are planting several garden spots, then perhaps one could contain a future large canopy tree as a replacement (nut, oak, pine). Otherwise, fruit woodland gardens focus on fruit trees: apple pear, mulberry, etc.

The companions for key species in a fruit woodland garden are often herbs, flowers, and berries. This could include raspberries, lemon balm, and bee balm. Remember, diversity adds beneficial functions for your garden, like pollinator habitat through the year. A fruit woodland spot can have companion plants within its 5' by 5' area, but these garden spots also work well with other edible ecosystem spots, such as berry meadows and prairie spots. Fruit woodlands are primarily useful as a source of food and recreation for humans, with a high output of edible products per square foot. For inspiration, consider the wild fruit forests of Eurasia discussed earlier.

Guild Example

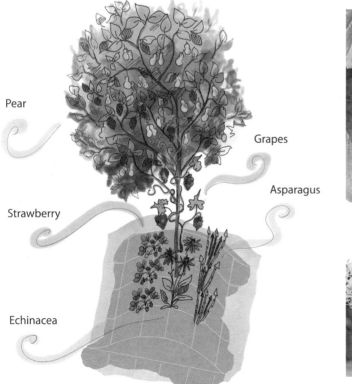

Pear

Grapes

Asparagus

Strawberry

Echinacea

Prairie Ecosystem: Goal = Restoration of Endangered Ecosystem

Guild Example

Prairie ecosystems have a mixture of grasses, sedges, fruits, herbs, and other flowering plants. They don't contain large woody plants but can be designed in your yard or other greenspaces in association with fruit woodland spots to form a more layered and diverse macro-landscape. Prairie ecosystems are valuable for land restoration, carbon sequestration, pollinator habitat, and medicinal plants. Prairie plants are useful for humans as medicine and as a source of food, fiber for basketry, and seeds (for further restoration of large landscapes of this most endangered ecosystem). Prairies are particularly effective in areas where pollinator species need special attention; consider a prairie spot if you are interested in ecosystem restoration and passionate about bee, butterfly, and other habitat creation.

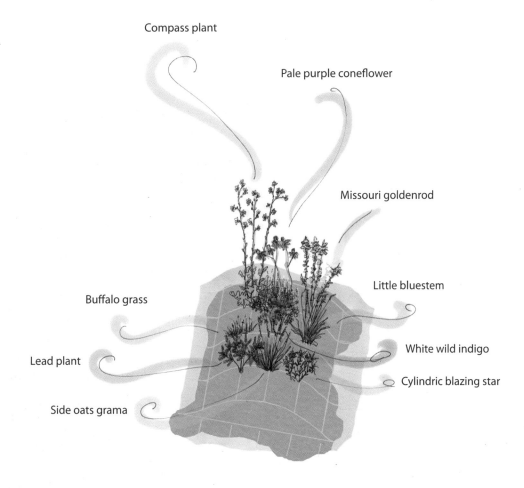

Compass plant

Pale purple coneflower

Missouri goldenrod

Little bluestem

Buffalo grass

White wild indigo

Lead plant

Cylindric blazing star

Side oats grama

Berry Meadow: Goal = Plant Propagation

Berry meadows are designed to mimic the productive meadow spaces that occur on the woodland edge, in disturbed forest environments (such as after a forest fire), or on the moorlands in Scotland. Berry meadows are sun-drenched spaces with a lot of productivity in the groundcover and bush layers. These spaces are great for stewards who wish to have yields of food quickly, as berries will produce well within 2–3 years. As such, these sites also stimulate interest, recreational value, and easy propagation for land transition elsewhere. One of the key goals for this example design is plant propagation (the production of new plants for landscaping). Meadow species are generally fast-growing and easy to propagate. As such, berry plants, such as raspberry or currants, are easy to propagate from cuttings and suckers (see next section), and berry meadow spots can be very effective catalysts for neighborhoods land transition due to high production of new plants with low labor and cost. Consider a berry meadow spot if your goal is to share new plants with your community or even to set up a part-time nursery with spring plant sales.

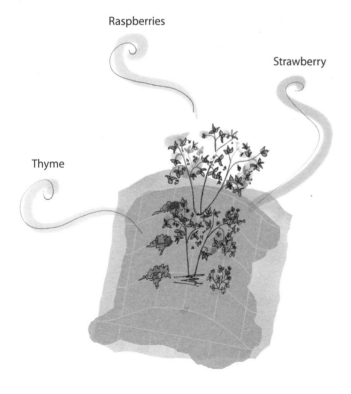

Modular
Ecosystem Landscape

To make sense of the landscape and achieve success in our efforts, we turn to organized patterns for design, planting, and maintenance, as well as short and long-term benefits.

Pattern to the Max

Patterns exist everywhere in nature and in our cultural designs. From the alternating tiles of a patio to the weaving of a blanket, humans create patterns readily, and we can use this sense of design to help us mimic wild ecosystems for human landscape design. Different guild spots can be arranged adjacent to each other in a pattern to form garden beds—a macro-landscape that functions as a whole. This can produce landscape designs such as edible hedges or larger food forests, and more. Patterned designs that alternate different ecosystems—such as a fruit woodland, a berry meadow, and a prairie—maximize yield and manage accessibility across the entire landscape. But before we start patterning different ecosystem guilds into larger ecological landscapes, we need to increase the space available for design.

Like the colors of this weaving from Guerrero, Mexico, we can blend different plants into a guild spot—and different guilds into a longer garden bed in an arranged pattern.

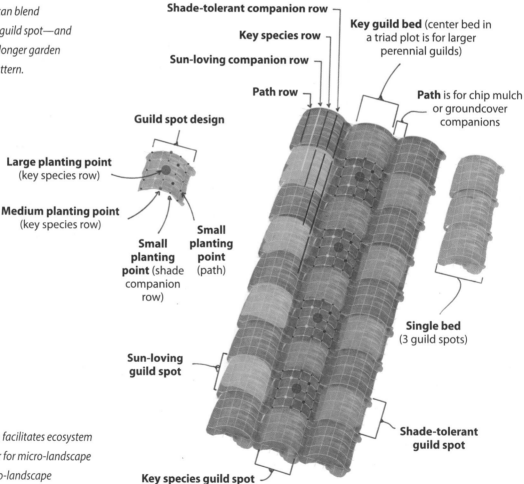

The Permabed System facilitates ecosystem design and is modular for micro-landscape beginnings and macro-landscape continuations.

Spots Become Beds

So far, we have been primarily discussing ecosystem spots—but how do we transition more land to edible biodiversity? Three or more 25 square foot garden spots linked together become a garden bed. Micro- and macro- are relative prefixes for landscape scope. However, for more precise discussion going forward, micro-landscapes are areas the size of a *single garden spot* or a single garden bed, and a macro-landscapes are sites that are turned into *multiple beds* or *plots*. Several micro-landscapes put together can become an ecosystem macro-landscape. Also, a linear edible ecosystem landscape can also be called an edible hedgerow. This distinction is made because many community sites will be suitable for a linear edible landscape, similar to our common hedges, but with edible plants and their own designation and design.

Beds Become Triad Plots

We can take garden spots and build beds, and three beds together make a macro-landscape, or garden plot. *The Permabed System* calls these *Triad Plots,* three beds together. A Triad Plot is a useful design unit for macro-landscapes. As a basic unit of design, it can be expanded to entire farm-scale production (see *The Permaculture Market Garden*). Again, **Planting Point, Guild Spots, Garden Beds,** and **Triad Plots** are the basic scales of edible ecosystem spatial management.

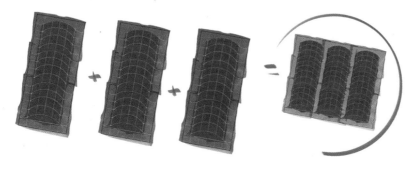

Triad Plot Design

These three-bed plots (Triad Plots) are very effective for designing efficient edible guilds. As soon as a grower has multiple adjacent beds under management, each bed becomes its own unit of management. Stewards can choose to plant guild spots within a bed according to an overall goal for the garden bed, such as *accessibility.* As soon as you manage a macro-landscape, you need to improve access for people, carts, and larger projects, such as small tractors. This bed will not only be productive, yielding herbs and providing pest confusion, it will also serve for efficient garden management because the low-growing groundcover design allows for easy access to the inner bed, with the key food plant species (such as fruit trees).

From irrigation to weeding, accessibility for people, tools, and equipment is crucial, and it comes down to elbow room and the ability for a cart or tractor to pass over a bed (possible for plants like thyme, strawberries, etc.). The cart tires can roll on the shoulder of the bed, and the tractor wheels can go in the path. You even have enough room to set up a ladder beside the groundcover bed to facilitate fruit harvest (this would be difficult if both companion beds had bushes).

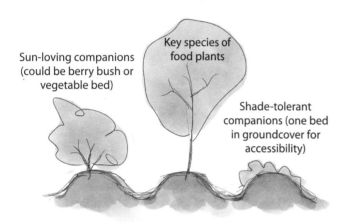

Sun-loving companions (could be berry bush or vegetable bed)

Key species of food plants

Shade-tolerant companions (one bed in groundcover for accessibility)

Having a design that enhances access to your food plants for management—weeding and harvest, in particular—is very important. Having low-growing plants adjacent to bigger trees greatly enhances accessibility when fruit is ready. This is also applicable in large landscape beds; for example, a bed of asparagus adjacent to a bed in fruit can improve accessibility to both. The asparagus is harvested in spring and will be mowed by the time the fruit is ready. This allows the steward to put a ladder over the asparagus to easily access the fruit harvest.

Alternating Layers

We can also create patterns when different garden spots are placed next to each other as a garden bed. We are patterning ecosystems by alternating the type of edible ecosystem by ecological layer: tree, bushes, herbs, etc. We want to space treed garden spots with a berry or prairie garden spot in between to give the tree room to grow and allow the plants to better partition resources. This layering is what creates a woodland edge landscape.

Alternating the layers of an ecosystem maximizes ecological productivity— the capacity of the system to photosynthesize, sequester carbon, and produce useful yields.

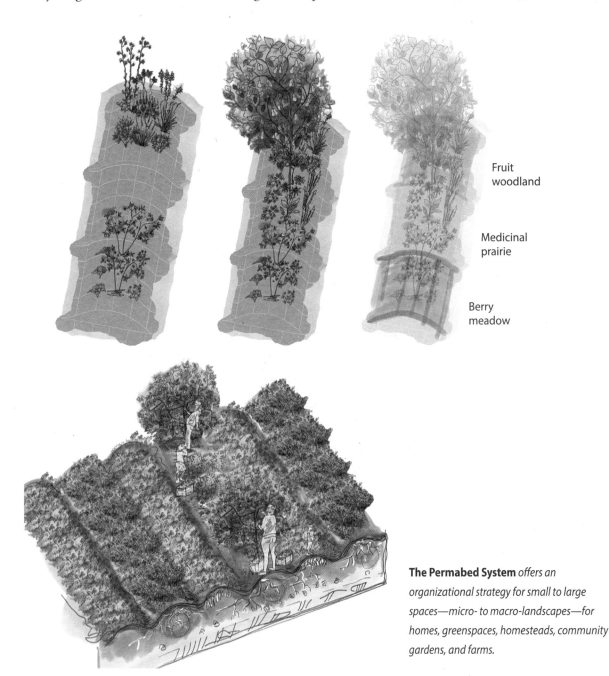

Fruit woodland

Medicinal prairie

Berry meadow

The Permabed System *offers an organizational strategy for small to large spaces—micro- to macro-landscapes—for homes, greenspaces, homesteads, community gardens, and farms.*

Bed Types

There are many different types of garden beds you can turn into edible ecosystems. Improvising with what you have, and the context of your garden space will help you find the right solution for you and your spot. The following are some examples and reasons for their design.

Planters can be made from galvanized horse troughs and other standard containers, making fast and simple garden beds where there isn't access to soil. Urban gardens and public spaces can benefit from this model.

Hügelkultur beds can be made using woody debris and other garden waste and home compost to build a raised bed with a long-term fertility source.

Moveable box garden beds can be made out of wood and an interior liner and built on pallets. In commercial applications, these can be built quite large, and forklifts used when the plants need to be brought in for the winter.

Raised-earth beds are easy to build, require no extra materials, and can be simply managed with common garden tools and good time-management techniques. They can also be easily expanded or added to.

Wood-siding beds can be very tidy in areas with limited space. However, a big drawback is the effective management of weeds because of all the "edge" between wood and soil; weeds prosper there, out of reach of a hoe or mower.

Even those without access to a yard, in a dense urban area, can have edible ecosystem abundance. This balcony garden in Mexico was home to dwarf fruit trees, herbs, and vegetables in pots.

Planters *can be made from galvanized horse troughs and other standard containers, making fast and simple garden beds where there isn't access to soil. Urban gardens and public spaces can benefit from this model.*

Moveable box garden beds *can be made out of wood and an interior liner and built on pallets. In commercial applications, these can be built quite large, and forklifts used when the plants need to be brought in for the winter.*

*Your property can become an **Edible Eden**.*

Section 4

Educate, Propagate, Inspire

ANY EDIBLE MICRO-LANDSCAPE CAN INFLUENCE ITS SURROUNDINGS to help transition other landscapes to edible ecosystem abundance, and so transform our society for the better. Dispersal, such as windblown dandelion seeds, is inherent to all ecosystems and needed for successful plant population establishment. Humans have always dispersed our favorite food plants. This section presents a model for community change that is based on the age-old mechanism of dispersal, both natural and human. Dispersal of site-suitable edible ecosystems results in the creation of new, edible micro-landscapes in your yard or your neighbor's. The key principles of **Education, Propagation, and Inspiration (EPI)** guide stewards in their ability to influence this positive change in their neighborhood. Following a special checklist of steps, any property can become an *EPI site* with an enhanced role as a *living laboratory* for research, *source point* of dispersal, and an *edible diversity hot spot*. Part of this checklist includes the *Permabed System* for Edible Ecosystem Design described in the previous chapter and the rest will follow in this section.

Ecosystem Dispersal

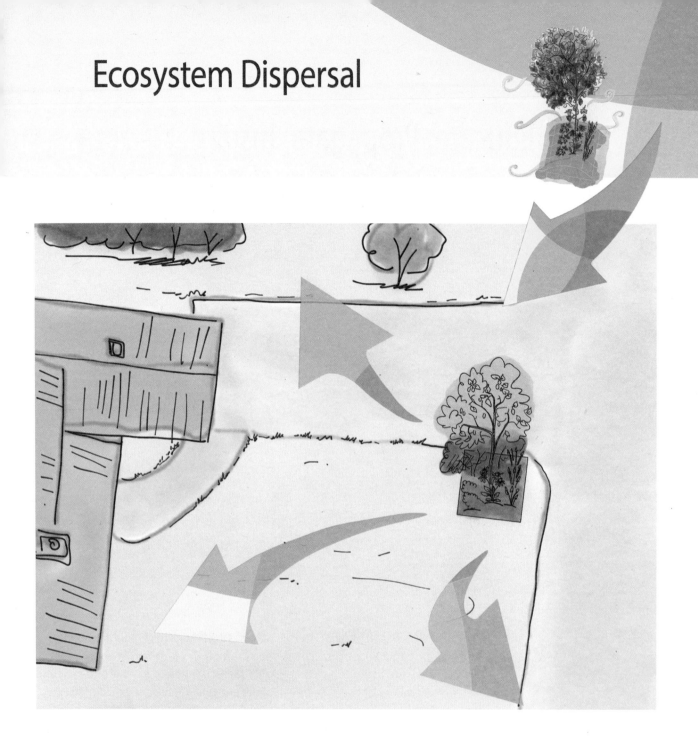

Now let's move outward from this piece of habitat we have sited, designed, and planted. Our gardens can spread across our yards and community greenspaces through the age-old mechanism of dispersal. From one edible ecosystem spot to another, we transition community landscapes.

Dynamic Ecosystems

A finished garden spot will become a dynamic micro-ecosystem with time. It will regenerate and regulate fertility, water, and pests. Ecosystems are not stagnant. They change, regenerate, evolve, and spread. A micro-ecosystem will have a natural tendency toward succession, creating new habitat within its zone of influence by affecting microclimate, soil, and water and providing new plant material in the form of seeds, suckers, and spores. As your garden plants set seed, new plants will grow, and the overall ecosystem genetic diversity will increase.

Spreading Success

One of the tendencies of ecosystem gardens is their capacity to spread. Natural ecosystems spread. Plants spread. This is an eco-logical principle! Successful plants and ecosystems are suitable for an area and well-adapted to their environment. Your spreading ecosystem will push up suckering raspberries, drop herbaceous seed, and send out strawberry runners. Successful ecosystems grow.

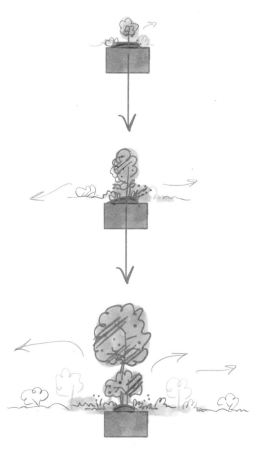

*The dynamic nature of your garden is the cornerstone for how you can begin to change your property or your community. **Success spreads!** An ecosystem can occur at all scales and grow to fill environments through dispersal of successful complements of organisms.*

An Apple Seed Becomes a Grove

A few plants can help create an entirely new ecosystem. Take the apple, for instance. A bird flying over the ancient apple forest of Eurasia might eat some fruit and fly away with a few seeds in its gut. These few seeds get dropped, along with a bit of avian manure, as a fertile little seed ball in the next valley.

Then, one seed produces one tree, another seed produces a second tree. The trees grows, seasons pass, they flower, pollination occurs, and fruit ripens and falls. A few seeds within a decade become a tree producing hundreds of apples—and each apple has its own complement of seeds. The individual trees will create a grove, and the grove can grow to become a forest. One a bird will carry a few seeds over the mountain to the next valley. This is natural dispersal.

One seed becomes a forest. What can natural dispersal teach us about how we can make change in our communities?

Natural Dispersal

All organisms disperse. Plants are well-known for using different mechanisms to disperse their seeds, including windblown (dandelion), mechanical launching of seeds (poppy), adhering to passing animals (burdock), being digested and moved in the animal's gut (apples).

Like a dandelion blowing in the wind, a single plant can become a colony, and a single garden can grow to be a landscape.

Garlic bulbils produced on the author's homestead are grown out to provide disease-free seed stock because they grow from the aerial part of the plant and are not exposed to soil-borne disease.

*Management of an ecosystem's natural tendency to spread provides a **cost-effective means of transitioning** our community greenspaces. This results in affordable and efficient manifestation of edible diversity benefits in our cultural landscape: a win-win for ecosystem and human community.*

Seeds of Diversity

Dispersal requires propagation. Plants have many different mechanisms for natural propagation, including seeds and suckers. There are benefits to both seed and vegetative propagation. Plants from seed have more genetic variability due to cross-pollination between different parent plants. Similar to siblings within a family carrying traits from both of their parents with lineage from each side of the family, they are similar in some respects and different in others. This provides the progeny with greater variability for survival within new and changing environments. The taller child will do better at basketball, perhaps, and the shorter one may be a pro at hide-and-seek. By evolution, if these games were a question of life and death, these traits could result in new species, with time. Certainly, a population of plants as a whole is more adaptable to environmental changes with a *diverse gene pool*. This genetic variability within an ecosystem is part of the resilience provided by biodiversity, and propagation using cross-pollination is a big part of this.

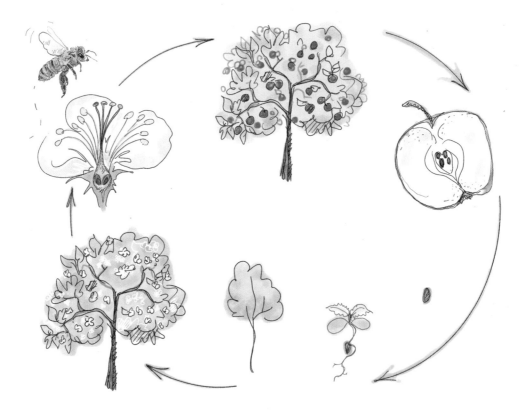

Bees moving from flower to flower carry pollen from different individual trees to pollinate flowers and produce genetically diverse seeds.

Suckers for Savings

On the other hand, vegetative clones can be dispersed very quickly, yielding larger plants sooner. These plants are more capable of fruiting earlier than a plant started from seed. Imagine a society that wished to select for only *basketball players* or only those suitable for successful *hide-and-go-seek*. We could do so more easily with clones, as was the case in one of the *Star Wars* movies, where a whole army was efficiently cloned from an ideal human specimen. However, this army is vulnerable in all the same ways too. Starting from seed provides variability that may be desirable in terms of resilience in case of pests, disease, and climate change, but it is a slower means of reproduction than cuttings and clones.

Diversity = Adaptability to Change

The genetic diversity of a seed from a pollinated flower is what helped make apple trees at home in a new environment in North America. When apples came *across the pond*, the seeds of the many cultivars brought over were spread across America, and the variability of their genetics brought on a wave of new varieties. Of all the seeds and all the trees that sprung up, the ones most suitable were selected regionally and became the heirloom varieties of apples America is known for. At one point, according to Dan Bussey, author of the *Illustrated History of Apples*, there were over 18,000 varieties![1]

The gene pool is the sum total genetic variability available to the population of a given species. All food plants have a local, regional, and even global gene pool we can draw upon for plant breeding. The bigger the gene pool, the more desirable traits available to improve varieties for drought tolerance, disease resistance, and cold hardiness—among others benefits for agriculture and society.

Dispersal Changes Communities

Both humans and nature can work side by side to change yards and communities to a new land-use diversity and composition. Humans have always dispersed edible and useful plants. We should continue to do this, keeping genetic diversity as a key principle in our propagation, dispersal, and land-use designs.

Both natural dispersal, such as wind-dispersed seeds, and human dispersal, from plant propagation, can change the landscape of a community. Together, nature and humans can work hand-in-hand to transition our landscapes to edible abundance.

A single strawberry can fill 25 square feet over a few years through natural dispersal, or the runners can be separated to start entirely new patches.

Propagation 101

The main means of propagating your food plants is through seeds, suckers, and scion wood. However, we can also divide rhizomes, split root systems, and collect spores.

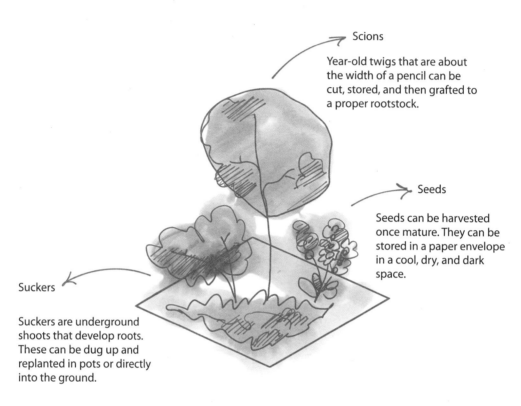

Scions

Year-old twigs that are about the width of a pencil can be cut, stored, and then grafted to a proper rootstock.

Seeds

Seeds can be harvested once mature. They can be stored in a paper envelope in a cool, dry, and dark space.

Suckers

Suckers are underground shoots that develop roots. These can be dug up and replanted in pots or directly into the ground.

All the layers of an edible ecosystem can be propagated through seed and/or vegetative means. Thyme and strawberry can be divided; grapes and raspberries can be propagated from suckers; and cuttings from groundcover and trees can be grafted.

Spreading Your Plantings

Where possible, allow nature to spread your favorite plants. If we choose to have certain plants in our yards, then we are intentionally, by removing unwanted plants, making space for them to become the dominant species in our greenspaces. Plants will propagate themselves by fulfilling their natural life cycle. Allowing flowers to bloom and set seed will result in an abundance of chives (for instance), or providing room for raspberries to sucker can result in a widening of your edible hedge. Seeds can be picked up by animals and birds and pop up around your yard and in your community. It is important to do research about any food plants you are growing to ensure they are not an **invasive species** in your area. In the case of our suburban communities, however, we are mostly talking about outcompeting non-native lawns and ornamentals. But do use due diligence.

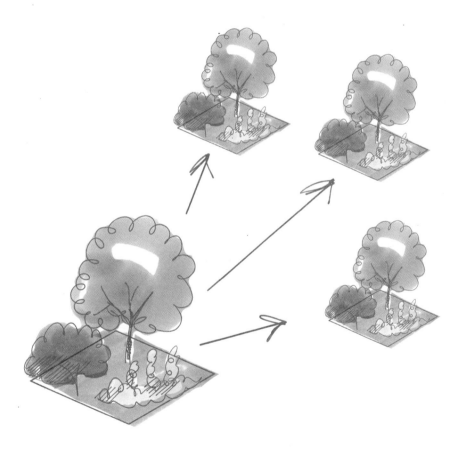

Successful guilds can be propagated to create new garden areas in your yard and community.

Edible
Ecosystem Qualities

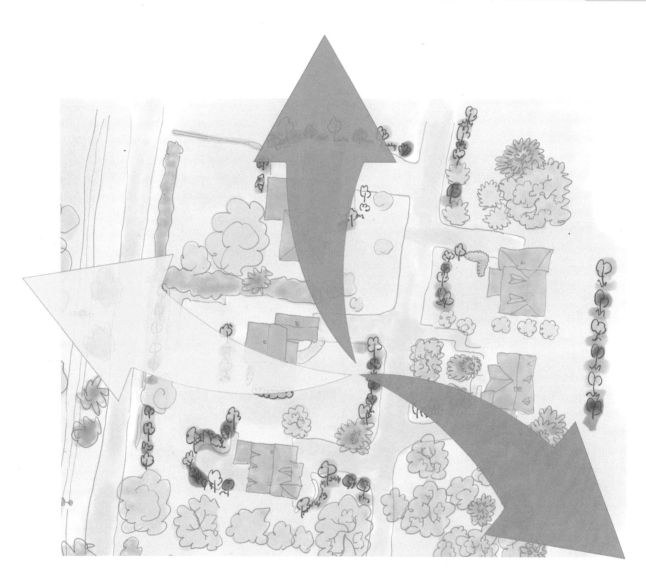

Let keep dispersing outward. *Your property can influence your neighborhood because it is capable of dispersing the ingredients for change.*

Hidden Treasures

Many of us look for worth and long-reaching value in what we do and how we spend our time and money. Your new edible ecosystem has *hidden treasures*. Yes, your garden has immense ecosystem services for you and your community—but, it also has real potential to transform the world! *Every drop of water makes the mighty ocean, and every edible micro-landscape transforms our society for the better.* What follows is a framework for affordable, efficient, and effective change of your neighborhood, region, and planet.

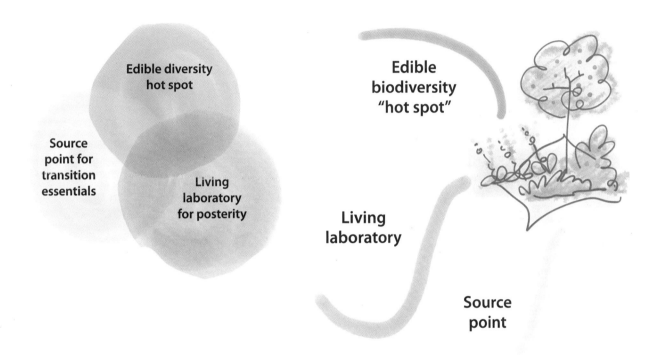

Your gardens are edible diversity "hot spots," living laboratories, and a source point for community transition.

Edible Diversity Hot Spot

Your property is a *repository of diversity*. The more you garden and landscape with edible and useful species, the more you are a steward of a *significant conservation area* within your neighborhood. Consider this: soon, you may have the most diverse property in your neighborhood, maybe in your city! What you have is something worthy of conservation and management.

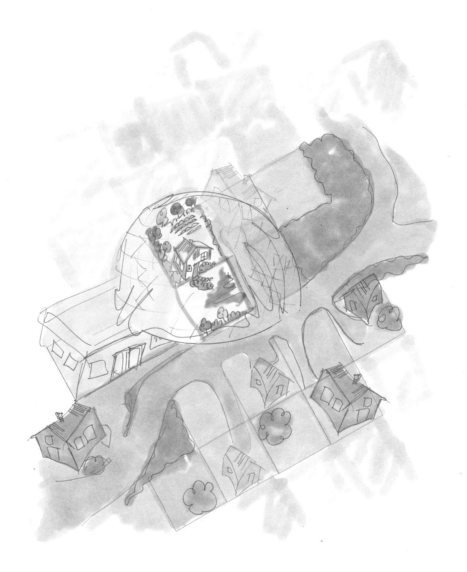

Global Diversity Hot Spots

The term *hot spot* refers to areas of high biodiversity. This can include wild biodiversity as well as agrobiodiversity. Costa Rica is considered a wild terrestrial biodiversity hot spot because it has one of the highest concentrations of endemic plant and animal species in the world. Mexico is also very biodiverse; although it is 1% of the world's land mass, it contains 10% of the world's biodiversity. Varied terrain and microclimates are partially to credit for this.

Mesoamerican Biodiversity Hot Spots

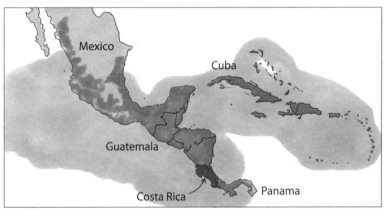

Highest

Medium

Lower

This is a map of regional biodiversity. Yellow shows areas that are relatively lower in biodiversity and red shows areas that are relatively the highest. Most all of Mesoamerica has high biodiversity, globally speaking.

Areas of food plant origin tend to be hotspots of agrobiodiversity; many of them still have ancestral food plants growing wild in remnant ecosystems. As recent as 2016, 61 genetically unique banana specimens were discovered in Papua New Guinea's Bougainville Island.[2] The banana industry is facing difficulties. The fruit is susceptible to disease because it has low genetic diversity—the result of thousands of years of clonal propagation and modern monoculture production. The significance of this banana diversity hot spot is a testimony to why we need to conserve our food heritage.

Security Is Diversity in Hand

As we have seen, biodiversity is a significant determining factor in societal success and collapse. The securing of diverse *ecosystems, plants,* and *genes* should be at the heart of modern socio-economic planning for both rural and urban sites. By planting and maintaining edible ecosystems with locally adapted and culturally significant varieties, we are *holding our diversity security near-to-home and close at hand.*

As Archimedes said in 300 BC, "Give me a firm spot on which to stand and I shall move the Earth."[3] With edible ecosystems, we can take a stand to secure the biodiversity that is in danger of being lost.

Rebuilding Agrobiodiversity

Because humans have lost much of our agrobiodiversity, your garden can be a space for rebuilding our genetic heritage. It has been a journey of thousands of years to create the agrobiodiversity we have today. Choosing heirloom fruits, berries, and herbs for your guilds is one way to revitalize and reinvigorate our food heritage. Choosing wild foodplants and recreating micro wild edible ecosystems is another option. Always, allowing your edible ecosystems to go wild, spread, and evolve will allow the genetic diversity to grow.

Landraces and wild food plants like those apple trees that have gone "feral" along fence lines in rural areas are a great treasure, and they are sources for rediscovering lost heirloom fruit varieties. We can turn these wild spots into edible diversity hot spots through design and management. We can create edible ecosystem spots around existing trees if they make a good key plant (see Section 3, "Edible Ecosystem Design").

As time passes, the plants in your ecosystem will produce new generations that will adapt to their environment. In this way, we can produce new landraces—locally adapted, genetically diverse, and useful plant varieties. Your edible ecosystem will evolve.

Living Laboratory

Any edible ecosystem can be considered a living laboratory. This means it is a space for study, experimentation, and demonstration. What will you do with the space you have? Is it ripe for living experimentation?

Lab for Land Transition

Your edible ecosystems are particularly effective as living laboratories for land transition in your community. Your gardens are experiments concerning the types of micro-landscapes available for transition, the food plants that may grow well in your area, and the guild companionship possibilities. Consider, for instance, an edible ecosystem that is developed in the median between a sidewalk and a road in an urban neighborhood. Or a spot that is making use of local wild food plants collected from an adjacent woodland. Or a community garden that is patterning perennial fruit trees with raspberries as a hedgerow along a perimeter fence line. One of the essential qualities of edible ecosystems is that they play uniquely with local conditions and possibilities. We can manage our gardens as living laboratories by actively seeking solutions and opportunities for our community under the role of **citizen scientists**.

Citizen Scientist

Every steward is a citizen scientist. The work you are doing in your garden is much more than growing healthy food and building a beautiful yard. The significance of what a garden truly is, its hidden treasure, can generate important scientific, cultural, and *agro-ecological* data. If a favorite plum tree is growing well, surviving the winters, is healthy, is yielding abundantly—this is important data for your community and may have even more significance down the road, when correlated with data from others.

Regional Food Plant Potential

Discovering which food plants, especially perennials, can grow well in your community is one of the most powerful tools for social change. Knowing our regional food plant potential through living testimony (as edible guilds growing in our yards) gives us the data we need to confidently transition more and more spaces to edible ecological abundance. One of the main goals of the living laboratory is to determine site-suitable food plant guilds.

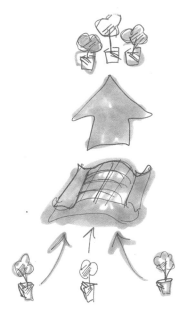

If you want to maximize your role as a citizen scientist, consider a good garden journal, excel at keeping record sheets, and share your data when opportunities present themselves. Having metal-etched tags is critical to make sure the plant varietal names are always intact and in situ.

Plants entering your property are assembled as a guild and trialed for site-suitability. Data-sharing can be as simple as telling your neighbors and encouraging them to plant a specific guild that is very successful or contributing your variety survival rates to a database for more widespread information exchange.

Site-Suitable Guilds

Determining site-suitability of a food plant and an entire guild is a process of checking off different key requirements. Plants come in from different sources—a neighbor, nursery, or seed catalog—*and it is your site* that demonstrates that they are actually suitable to your community. No matter the sticker tag claims, the best guilds are ones that demonstrate through the long-term that they are site-suitable.

Site-suitable guilds should meet the following requirements:

1. **They survive.** The plant should be able to survive its soil, moisture, and climatic conditions for at least three years, and they must demonstrate **hardiness**. Plant hardiness is based on average winter temperatures for a region and a variety's ability to survive these conditions. Hardiness maps delineate continents into planting zones to help us understand which perennials will survive the winter. Nursery and seed catalogs will tell you a plant's hardiness, and hardiness maps can be found for most areas on a regional scale. If, for instance, a particular variety of peach survives in your yard over several winters, this tells you it can survive the winter lows in your hardiness zone.
2. **They are successful.** The garden design, bed layout, and management style must be successful and meet the goals of the design. Otherwise, the garden is weedy, or plants succumb to disease or drought. A measure of success is the ease of management to meet desired outcomes.
3. **They are sensational.** The food plant guild must yield a bounty of food, provide beauty, and be a source of wonderful sights and smells. Essentially, if the guild is joyful to your five senses, then it is sensationally suitable.

Image credit: USDA plant hardiness zone map 1990

Part of our role as citizen scientists is testing the boundaries of hardiness zones and revealing new food plant potential in regions where fruit trees, berries, and herbs might grow but haven't been thoroughly tested in a changing climate.

Site Suitable
=
✓ Survival.
+
✓ Successful.
+
✓ Sensational.

The data gathered on the small scale can be very relevant for large acreage restoration through multi-scale collaboration. Integrating prairie meadows in our ditches and property fronts provides great habitat, stormwater regulation, and carbon sequestration. Collaborating with other landowners can lead to greater benefit through spreading seeds, ideas, and inspiration to farms and public spaces.

Source Point

Every plant is a source of seeds, suckers, or scions. Each garden spot is a point of edible ecological dispersal. Edible ecosystems are essentially epicenters of land transition through both natural and human dispersal of their successful guild plants and designs. They are also source points of ecosystem benefits to the community, and their services spread with each new spot that is planted. Each garden has what is needed to create new gardens in your community.

A yield of delicious disease-free fruit is a good indication of sensational suitability.

Disperse Site-Suitable Guilds

If your guilds are site-suitable, then they are also suitable to be dispersed throughout your community and into communities elsewhere. This means your individual plants can be dispersed through propagation of seeds, suckers, and scions, or the food plant guild as a whole can be propagated and emulated elsewhere as a replica of the original guild.

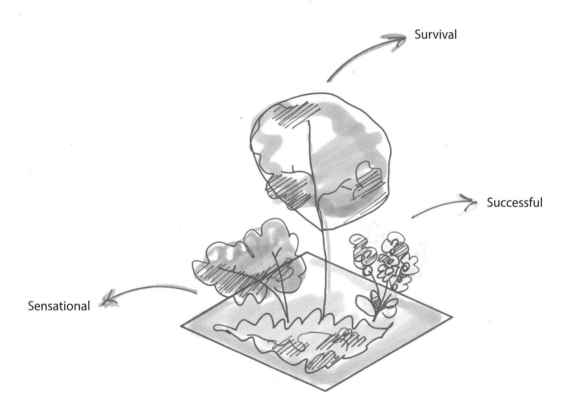

A site-suitable guild is replicated because its plants are individually successful, sensational, and survive—but when a guild meets these criteria as a companionship unit, this is even more worthy of dispersal for land transition elsewhere.

Catalyzing Land Transition

Lets continue to disperse outward into this neighborhood—any neighborhood. Your ecosystem garden has the capacity to influence its immediate surroundings; it is a catalyst for transitioning land. In this way, one yard can influence those nearby.

What Is Needed to Transition?

To transition our community greenspaces using dispersal of site-suitable guilds, we need a mechanism for catalyzing community members and ensuring their success. What is needed so that the diversity we conserve, trial, and disperse is successfully implemented on other properties and greenspaces? In order to find the answer, we can look to the past to see how humans have transitioned land, and we can mimic their strategies to catalyze the change we want to see today.

How We Changed Land

Humans have been changing the land for hundreds of thousands of years and quite extensively in the last 10,000 years. We did it as many individuals and societies, and yet it was collectively governed by three cultural phenomena:

1. **Inspiration.** We were inspired by wild ecosystems and later cultural landscapes that were abundant, beautiful, and useful, and we acted on this inspiration to have more of it.
2. **Propagation.** We harvested, saved, and propagated this diversity and spread it where we lived.
3. **Education.** Every food plant has its own needs, and successful care, breeding, and propagation required the sharing of knowledge.

Ecosystem biodiversity inspired and informed early humans, teaching us and providing us with plants to propagate and disperse.

A single fruit tree, even old or neglected, can still yield hundreds of pounds of fruit, hundreds of scions, thousands of seeds, and demonstrate its site-suitability. Edible ecosystems "do their thing" without our intervention, including offering ecosystem services for the benefit of humanity and other life. They inspire us to enjoy them and obtain more of their benefits nearer to home.

Naturally So

An ecosystem, macro or micro, *naturally provides* education, propagation, and inspiration. Through stewardship, you can further its successful dispersal, but know that it will do this even without your intervention. It can passively **educate** through the fundamentals of its unique design; proffer plants, seeds, and scion wood through natural **propagation**; and offer a beautiful garden spot that will **inspire** neighbors.

Wild Homestead Catalyst

As an example of how an edible ecosystem can catalyze change naturally, consider these quintessential homestead favorites: rhubarb, apple, asparagus, horseradish, raspberry, and strawberry. Despite the loss of family farms, these plants still pop up near old homesteads and corners of barns; uncared for, they persist. People still spread (propagate) these abandoned patches into new garden spaces because their shoots and fruits are delicious (inspiration), and their hardiness and vigor show site-suitability (education).

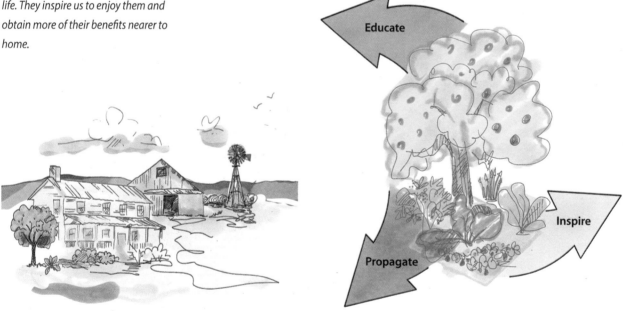

Land Transition Catalysts = Educate, Propagate, Inspire

Humans have always been educated from experiences on the land. We propagated the wild abundance around us, domesticated it, and continued to disperse this biodiversity by inspiring others with our landscape successes. If we build the capacity of our edible ecosystems to provide these catalysts, we enhance community land transition. One edible ecosystem can inform and provide the creation of another. Your neighbor passing by will be inspired by your garden. If they ask questions, you can provide them with plants and designs.

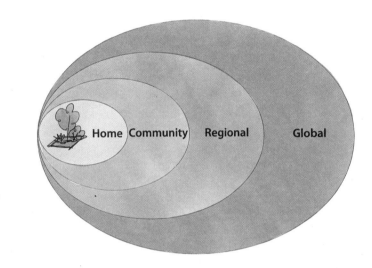

Land Transition Catalysts: (Education, Propagation, and Inspiration) facilitate effective and efficient creation of more successful edible ecosystem gardens. Anyone, anywhere, can radiate out the knowledge, plants, and inspiration to their neighbors.

EPI Is a
Model for Success

Now, we zoom out to this Montreal neighborhood, now transformed with many ecosystem spots. The EPI System is a framework for maximizing land transition catalysts (Education, Propagation, Inspiration) for successful land transition. Many EPI sites can make big changes.

What Is an EPI Site?

We aim to transform our society with increased ecosystem benefits by transitioning communities to edible diverse landscapes. Catalysts make this transition happen because they lower the amount of energy needed to activate change for desired results. **Land Transition Catalysts** provide community members with **education** of designs and techniques, **propagation** of successful edible varieties, and **inspiration** to act now to achieve ecosystem benefits. With these catalysts—Education, Propagation, and Inspiration (EPI)—we have a shorter road to travel to a much brighter, biodiverse future. Every edible ecosystem garden and its steward is a community resource and can become an **EPI** site—a space that maximizes land transition to ecosystem benefits.

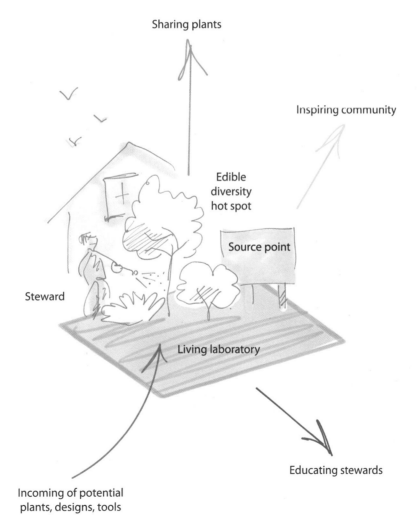

The first stage of being an EPI site is to have the essentials.

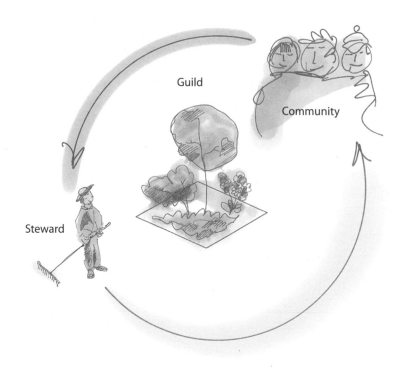

Of primary importance is:

1. a steward who is motivated to educate the public
2. a successful food plant guild to propagate
3. a community ready to be inspired

Stewards are moving and shaking their communities by setting an example and providing mentorship and sponsorship. Stewards can form core groups to transition and maintain community greenspaces.

Stewardship Roles

Stewardship is the care of our Earth. It is responsible action in connection with the source of our societal success and well-being. We are stewards of our land. Humans have traditionally been caretakers of the ecosystem within which we live. Care for your habitat, and it will reward you! But beyond your own needs, you are the steward of your land for your community, for posterity, and a powerful grassroots player in moving our world to a better place through landscape transition.

Stewardship

Setting an example (**exemplify**) is the easiest form of stewardship. Walk the talk, so to speak. The next form of stewardship is **mentorship**, or the sharing of knowledge with others on how to do what you do. The last form of stewardship is **sponsorship**, or the provision of direct support to others to allow them to become better stewards themselves. This can take the form of financial support, design assistance, and certainly the provision of site-suitable food plants you propagate. As you can see, the three types of stewardship enhance the three types of Land Transition Catalysts (E, P, and I).

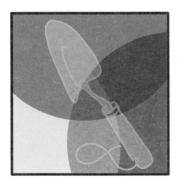
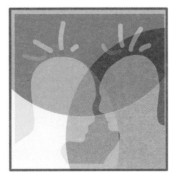

Exemplify   *Mentorship*   *Sponsorship*

EPI System

As we design our gardens, grow food, and share plants, we are effectively creating change in our community by helping catalyze land transition to edible biodiversity. However, we can *galvanize* our stewardship reach by following the **EPI System** and its protocol that is designed to maximize land transition success. This protocol is summed up as a checklist (see page 213) of steps taken to become a high-impact **EPI Site** that multiplies ecosystem benefits through influencing the creation of many more similar micro-landscapes.

The EPI System, developed by the Ecosystem Solution Institute, builds on the ecosystem benefits and land-use opportunities outlined in Sections 1 and 2 of this book, as well as the edible ecosystem design models presented in Section 3. Starting in Section 3 and into Section 4, the main EPI System principles were discussed, and they share the same checklist icons, as seen below, to help you reference these skills. The EPI System is scalable for micro- and macro-landscapes, as well as urban, suburban, or rural land use. It is meant to connect us all and help build biodiversity in our backyards and beyond.

The EPI Checklist

This **EPI CHECKLIST** is a prioritized list of key site components that maximize good site design, best management practices, and Land Transition Catalysts. Please note, this checklist is a continuum toward increasing your garden's capacity for land transition, but it always starts with simply planting a garden and caring for it. Yet, it is always good to have the ultimate goal in mind to help you get there! By following this Checklist, we can help manifest our garden's *high-impact potential* for changing the face of our communities for the better. For the full EPI Checklist, go to www.ecosystemsolutioninstitute.com.

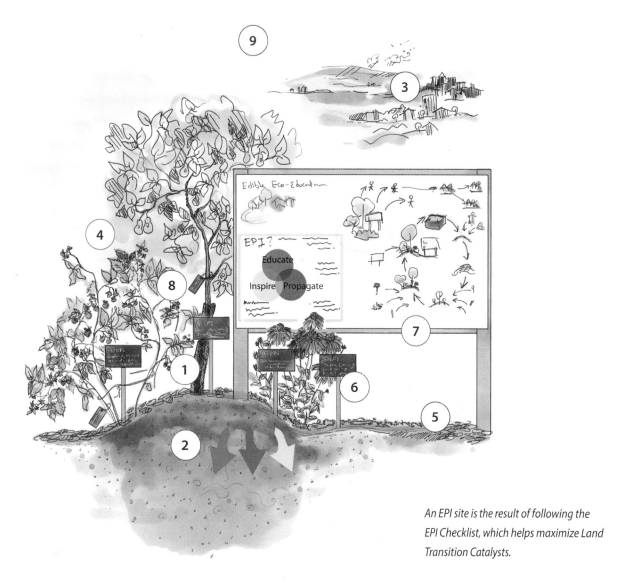

An EPI site is the result of following the EPI Checklist, which helps maximize Land Transition Catalysts.

 1. Site selection and analysis

 4. Design an ecosystem guild

 7. Educate your community

 2. Build a permabed

 5. Plant a micro-landscape

 8. Propagate the best plants

 3. Source site-suitable edible and useful plants

 6. Emphasize ecosystem qualities

 9. Inspire land transition and societal transformation

EDUCATION

A successful garden has everything needed to teach others to emulate it. Ecosystem garden spots can demonstrate how to prepare a site from scratch, how to plant, which plants are site-suitable, basic maintenance, and more. Community education can be enhanced through further knowledge exchange with the steward, the information on plant tags, and even an edible eco-education interpretative panel at some sites. This can be further enhanced through workshops or the use of social media. *Education is a Land Transition Catalyst because it gives people the knowledge they need to create edible ecosystems of their own.*

Signage, good record-keeping, and social media can help educate community transition.

PROPAGATION

The essence of propagation within the EPI System is simple: design guilds of site-suitable food plants, ensure they have durable name tags, and propagate your favorites. Spread successful plants to new garden spots on your property, propagate some more, share with neighbors. Maybe evolve your efforts to create a nursery and become a significant source of site-suitable food plants. *Propagation is a Land Transition Catalyst because it supplies the needed plants to fill the underutilized greenspaces of our communities with something better.*

Steward

Tags

Guild

EPI sites disperse site-suitable food plants into their yards and communities, and they can even form the basis of micro-enterprises.

Long-lasting name tags are integral to the EPI System, as it allows plant information sharing and maintains genetic data into the future better than typical nursery tags do. Many years later, even after a property changes hands, the living testimony of a plant's site-suitability can be connected to its name and influence community food security and resilience.

INSPIRATION

Inspiration is about getting a community to take action—encouraging neighbors to pick up shovels and make their own garden spots. If your edible micro-landscape is beautiful, abundant, diverse, delicious, and nutritious, then your neighbors will be inspired. Whether to keep up with the Joneses, or to enjoy in the ecological bliss, the beauty, and abundance is what brings them to your fence line.

"What is this?" they might ask.

"Have a try!" you say.

"Incredible. Your yard is so beautiful! We loved all the flowers in spring!"

"Well," you say with a grin. "I started with just 25 square feet!"

Inspiration is a Land Transition Catalyst because devoted and knowledgeable stewards who create effective micro-landscapes will rouse others to do the same.

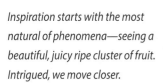

Inspiration starts with the most natural of phenomena—seeing a beautiful, juicy ripe cluster of fruit. Intrigued, we move closer.

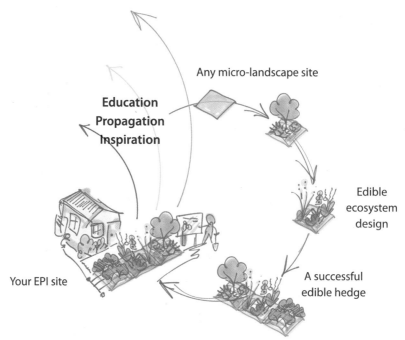

The EPI establishment cycle includes building your garden spot, trialing new guilds, maximizing land transition catalysts (E, P, and I), and dispersing into your community.

Any micro-landscape site

Education Propagation Inspiration

Edible ecosystem design

A successful edible hedge

Your EPI site

Section 5

Ecosystem Culture

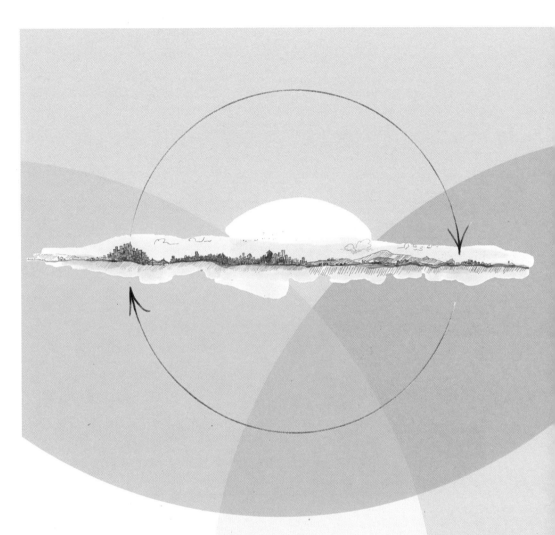

ECOSYSTEM CULTURE? WHAT DOES THIS MEAN? With everything said and depicted within these pages, it is clear ecosystems are fundamental to our society and to community health, wealth, and well-being. An **ecosystem culture** is one that *benefits from* and *supports* its diverse, edible, and useful abundance. An ecosystem culture nurtures its habitat, for its habitat provides for all socio-economic and cultural needs. What is more essential than ecosystem services or more practical than having them near-to-home? Transitioning our land to edible ecological abundance will change people through their contact with a traditional-modern habitat. By changing people, we transform our culture.

Transitioning Our Habitat

Shall we continue to disperse these ecosystem benefits outward and connect the urban and rural divide? Yes, the EPI communities influence their surroundings and bring about a transition to more diverse abundance and increased accessibility to this human habitat across broad landscapes.

Human Habitat Relationship

Transitioning land to edible ecosystems is part of the story of human evolution. We have always been inspired by nature, enjoyed ecosystem services, and maximized them through our land planning. Humans have been on a journey, from our early origins in wild, ancestral ecosystems, to the formation of cultural landscapes. But now, in modern times, we are undergoing a massive *loss* of biodiversity and ecosystem services. Our continued degradation of Earth's natural capital suggests we have *yet to discover our true potential as stewards* of the habitats that provide socio-economic success and community well-being. By integrating human habitation and ecosystem services, we can create direct relationships with our cultural landscape again and put their services front and center in our communities and decision-making. The EPI System is a roadmap to a future we know will be better. It can be a future of wealth and health, located right where people live—a **future of edible ecosystem abundance**.

Human relationships with the land are still evolving. Let's play an active, thoughtful part in these transitions.

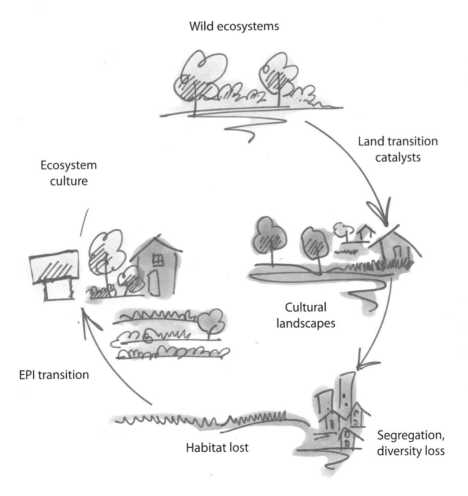

Wild ecosystems

Land transition catalysts

Ecosystem culture

Cultural landscapes

EPI transition

Habitat lost

Segregation, diversity loss

Wasted Spaces to Big Benefits

There is an abundance of space ready for transition to edible ecosystem benefits. EPI sites can pop up in any community, and any greenspace that is underutilized is an opportunity. When we open our eyes, we can begin to truly see the potential for change. There is no space too small. Many spaces make up the sum of change.

Here, various greenspaces in the city of Winnipeg are highlighted with colored circles to show the wealth of opportunities in underutilized spaces.

Community Succession

Once we begin to transition land, our community ecosystem will have its own socio-ecological succession. A natural ecosystem changes through ecological succession, and our edible ecosystem community will, as well. The trees, bushes, shrubs, vines, and herbs will mature and grow with time. More people will install even more edible ecosystem landscapes, adding to the spatial expansion of edible ecosystem abundance. The ecosystems' species will evolve as seeds drop, new plants emerge, and the gene pool diversifies through cross-pollination and selective processes. There will be a change in species composition and, with time, abundance. Larger nut trees, sugar maples, and dominant fruit trees will form the canopy. Shade-tolerant herbs and medicinal plants will grow in the cool shadows, and the edges will be abundant with berries, like raspberry and currant, with many flowers in seasonal bloom, and other small fruit and nut trees, like plum and hazelnut, sharing their bounty in turn. Over time, the landscape will evolve, and the ecosystems themselves will grow in complexity and potential. Ecosystem services will be well rooted in our communities.

Human relationships with the land will change as new abundance emerges, as children grow up amidst this diversity, and as our routines are surrounded by the seasonal enjoyment and care of our new ecosystem community.

EPI Is for Anyone, Anywhere to Transition Land Use

The beauty of the transition model is that it can be done by *anyone, anywhere*. If we want to effect big change in our society, we need models that can be implemented by all of Earth's citizens or at least be as accessible as possible in all our socio-economic, environmental, and individual contexts. The EPI System has three key attributes that make it possible for anyone, anywhere, to succeed through their own means or sponsorship.

1. **Small Space.** Because EPI Sites only require micro-landscapes to be effective, they have low time, space, and energy costs. It is a scale that is approachable and less intimidating to new gardeners. These sites are also actionable because they require very little financial cost and few special tools. Finally, these sites are achievable because they are small enough to be completed rapidly in a reasonable amount of time.

2. **Site-Suitability.** Site-suitable design makes the EPI System a good approach to effect change because it is fundamentally a system for finding *what actually works right where you are* in terms of plants, tools, and designs. It works for any climate, landscape, or situation because *it is meant to be designed to suit.* Trial and error, local and traditional knowledge, and mimicry of a **model design*** can help anyone, anywhere, find a site-suitable edible ecosystem spot.

3. **Natural Principles.** The EPI System is based on natural principles, and natural principles govern our success. Wherever you are, if your food plant guild is successful, it will spread. Seeds and suckers will disperse, and the guild will grow. It is also human nature to emulate what is great. If your guild is beautiful and abundant, people will approach and learn and try their own edible ecological spots. Part of the applicability of this system is that it relies on natural principles for its design, and *this is sound design management.*

* A "model design" is any design you learn from another gardener or expert and adopt and adapt to your situation. EPI is a model design for catalyzing land transition. Similarly, this book presents model designs for different types of edible ecosystem guilds, including medicinal prairies, fruit woodlands, and berry meadows.

Land, People, Culture

Let's zoom out to see that across this city (any city), and the surrounding countryside, many communities act as hot spots, source points, and living laboratories to create an ecosystem culture. Landscape transition manifests a cultural paradigm shift over time.

New Paradigm

Rather than focusing on being green or not green, pro-industry, or against, we can focus on regenerative edible ecosystems services. Yet, the *long-term stability* of edible ecosystems depends on ecological land-planning, maintenance, and policy. And this, in turn, depends on our **cultural values,** which ultimately govern personal, community, and political decision-making. Without a *cultural shift* to global understanding, respect, and prioritizing of sustainable ecosystem management, we may slip back into the doldrums, deficits, and dangers of unsustainable, extraction-based socio-economics and the culture that supports it. *Human culture has always been formed from the land.* The land—the environment, the ecosystems we interacted with as early people—changed us. It tested us, inspired us, beckoned us to taste, care for, and breed its rich abundance. We prospered and designed. We can merge this ancestral tendency and our modern knowledge to bring about a new paradigm of community well-being and societal resilience.

We can go places we have never been while honoring our origin and the constraints of our planet's biocapacity.

The Value of Use or Exchange

It is worth understanding "value" better because our society must appreciate ecosystem services holistically in order to support them directly. This can be analyzed from two sides: **the value of use** (we enjoy a livable planet) and **the value of exchange** (we buy and sell goods). Although we *use* much of what we exchange (eating the food we buy), *we don't always buy what we use* (breathing air, drinking water, enjoying livable temperatures).[1] Therein lies the rub, for we often degrade natural capital through the *industry of exchange* and so harm our use of ecosystem goods and services that are critical, but not bought or sold.

For instance, our global food system is dependent on monoculture agriculture, long-distance shipping, and toxic inputs that impact biodiversity. Essentially, the conditions of a livable planet (air, water, temperatures, ecological productivity) are *mostly free,* yet our current socio-economic model limits the long-term truth of this statement because of pollution, ecosystem degradation, and biodiversity loss.

Billions of Services

Understanding ecosystem services has been at the forefront of science for several decades. The services ecosystems provide us have been valued at billions of dollars. They are immeasurably necessary to societal success and resilience in the face of the socio-economic and environmental changes the world will continue to face in this century. Every spot of suburban yard, urban boulevard, and acre of farm country contributes to the local, regional, and global ecosystem services we benefit from. Yet, there is still underutilized, uniform, and organized land to implement ecosystem design efficiently within our cultural landscape. There are benefits to find in every biome and every region, and in every spot that a steward will make a stand in and plant an ecosystem spot.

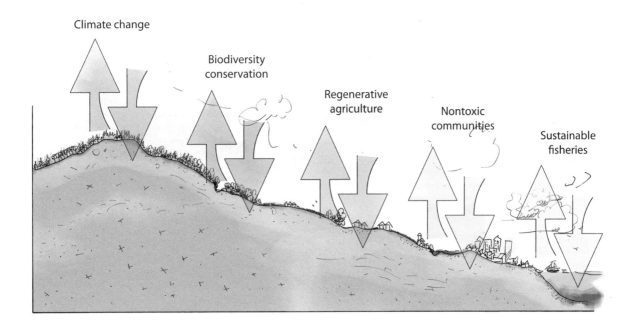

Every space in our cultural landscape is a place where we, as stewards, can create ecosystems that interact productively with Earth's life-support systems on which our health and wealth depend.

Ecosystem Economy

We need to see a shift toward increasingly valuing **ecosystem use** (like clean air) at the same time as prioritizing **ecosystem exchange** (such as local fruit) over other economic activity. For instance, edible hedges in our neighborhoods could be understood and valued for the far-reaching, multi-purpose, and resilient benefits they provide. At the same time, we also need to prioritize increasing the value of the exchange of ecosystem services over other cultural services; essentially, we must rebuild an ecosystem economy. Designing these edible hedges and entire communities to have pathways to profit from their ecosystem services will keep them front and center in land-use planning over other demands for community space. The demand for local, niche, and specialty food, eco-experiences, and other products and services that edible ecosystems can provide is key to improving the exchange value of edible ecosystem landscapes. The tourist value, for instance, of the first truly edible city will be mind-boggling!

A well-designed edible landscape highlights the value of ecosystem uses and maximizes its value of exchange. Edible bike lanes, like this one in Montreal, are a gateway to rebuilding a green economy and community wellness through vibrant community spaces that reduce the community's ecological footprint, create green jobs, and attract new tourism.

Transition Land

How do we bring about this shift? Again, we can look to natural principles and our evolution in ecosystems as a viewfinder for how to achieve cultural change. Our ancestral experiences within ecosystems are the source of land transition catalysts which fundamentally helped form our cultural landscapes and who we are today. By marrying these *origin facts* with our modern understanding of ecosystem services, we can *let the land lead us again*, but this time we need to shift to a new socio-economic paradigm. What better point to lead an ecosystem renaissance than by transitioning our cultural landscape until it reaches a sufficient scale of biodiversity to transform our culture? Little by little, one spot at a time, we can begin the journey. The land will be so irresistible it will cause people to change to a new cultural understanding. Be ambitious and make your mark. It is a worthwhile project to transition a spot of land!

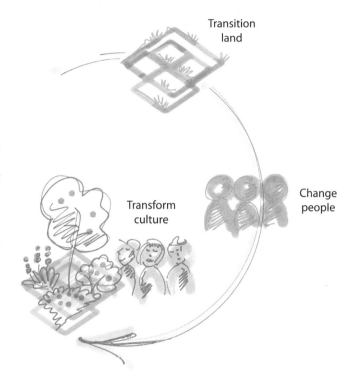

"Individual ambition serves the common good."

— Adam Smith [2]

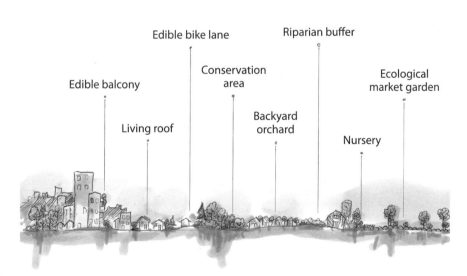

Gardens can exist on balconies, in city parks, or in abandoned parking lot edges. We build the future we want to see by maximizing the spaces around us. Stand up in your neighborhood and reclaim your underutilized, inefficient greenspaces. Every spot counts.

Change People

As the land transitions to edible ecological abundance, people will begin to change. As flowers bloom, people will smell them; as berries ripen, people will taste them; as the leaves change and fall, people will see them. As the land evolves and increases in abundance, people will harvest, share, and store it. Ecosystems will provide benefits to humans where they live. We will grow healthier from the nutrition, the activity, the community. *We will care for the land.* Our air and water will become cleaner, and we will be better for it. There will be change in human health: lower anxiety in diversified green-spaces at work, improved childhood intelligences from edible schoolyards, and enhanced nutrition in communities of all kinds. As the land changes, people change.

The changes in the land will result in a new sort of community—a community full of the songs of birds, the flutters of butterflies, and the green, growing reach of trees. The community will be full of the life of turtles and foxes and children at play.

Transform Culture

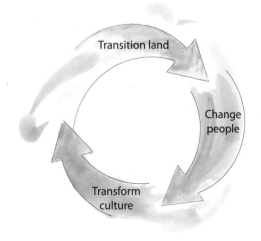

As people change, culture is transformed. Culture is the threshold of our society's home on Earth—it is how we frame our "understanding of things" over generations. With this transformation we will celebrate seasonal abundance, value the services of the ecosystem communities, and maintain their functioning purposefully. We will appreciate the farmers who feed us from their diverse farms, building soil, conserving carbon, and investing in our truly sustainable future. Our cultural values will cement the edible ecological landscape around us through sound *long-term land planning, management, and policy*. People will secure their ecosystems through more green jobs, valued ecological healthcare, and the recognition of resilience as fundamentally bound to biodiversity. Our culture is transformed through each generation that grows up with a biodiversity perspective and priority.

Ecosystem Culture

So, we *transition land to change people* and thus *transform our society* to an **ecosystem culture**—one that is edible, biodiverse, resilient, profitable, and healthy. This cultural transformation has two main aspects. First, the benefits of ecosystem goods and services are **near-to-home**. People live better lives when they live immersed in ecological spaces and have full access to multifunctional and sustainable wealth and well-being. Secondly, ecosystem cultures sustain habitats through **direct investment** in ecosystem services. Society is resilient through diversity; our economy upholds regenerative productivity, and human well-being is saturated in ecological healthcare.

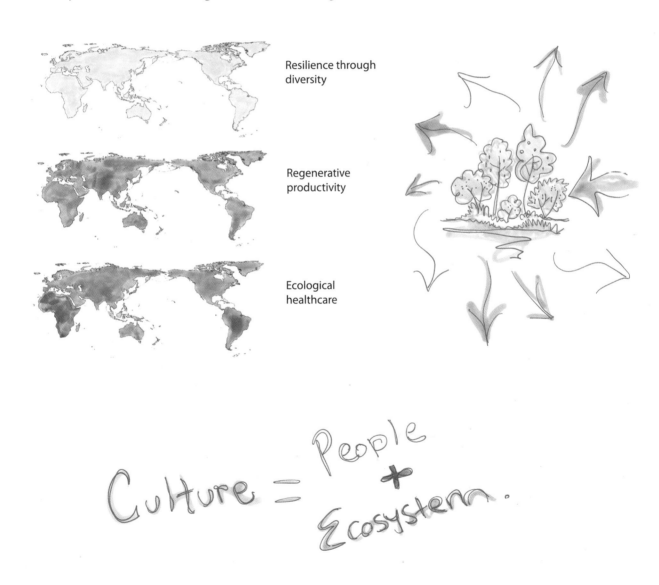

Resilience through diversity

Regenerative productivity

Ecological healthcare

Culture = People + Ecosystem.

Take Direct Action

It is no longer enough to assume that ecosystem services will always be there. Remember, we have left the planet's ecological grace period, and, at the current rate of biodiversity loss and ecosystem degradation, we are jeopardizing planetary life-support systems. Let's not misunderstand—the Earth will persevere, life will persist, evolution is a constant—the question is this: what about humanity? Will we persevere? And more importantly, what is the quality of life in our near future and for generations to come? Our ecological wealth and well-being are at risk now, and the benefits are ours to be had now. People, young and old, can take up arms through direct landscape action—a tree, and herb, and ecosystem spot.

Ecosystem culture would entail direct investment in ecosystem goods and services near to where we live—where biodiversity benefits can be most received, their security best held, and their stewardship best managed.

"We should preserve every scrap of biodiversity as priceless while we learn to use it and come to understand what it means to humanity."

—E. O. Wilson, *The Diversity of Life*

Services for Ecosystems

Now is the time to expand the understanding of ecosystem services and see how we can support our valuable ecosystems. Our relationship with ecosystem services can be seen as three-fold: 1) Services are provided **by** ecosystems, 2) Services are provided **to** ecosystems, and 3) Services are provided **within** an ecosystem.

We need to rebuild ecosystem integrity and so improve our societal success and resilience.

There are three key ways we can provide services for ecosystems in our modern landscape:

 1. **Diversify** current greenspaces.

 3. Create **more greenspaces** overall.

 2. **Increase the accessibility** of ecosystem services through integrating and connecting landscapes so people can enjoy and maintain them.

Essentially, we need more biodiverse, accessible ecosystem landscapes. With EPI, we do this directly by creating edible ecosystem landscapes that conserve biodiversity, find solutions for land use, and catalyze the transition of underutilized spaces in our communities.

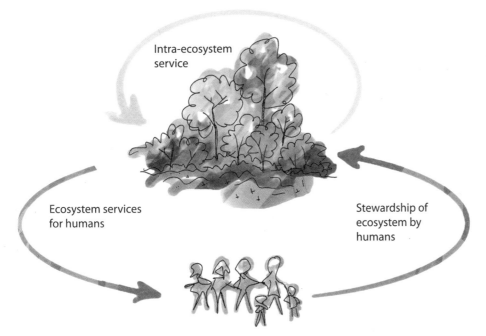

Intra-ecosystem service

Ecosystem services for humans

Stewardship of ecosystem by humans

We must directly support ecosystems so they can support themselves and support us.

Change Has Many Stakeholders

Now, as we continue to zoom out, *we see ecosystem culture is spreading across this region (any region) and people from all walks of life are influencing landscape transition and cultural transformation across a broad region. EPI is a multi-stakeholder approach to land transition.*

Many Stakeholders

There will be many stakeholders in the transition of our communities to edible ecosystem abundance. There are many who will benefit from this transition, and each has a unique role to play. Every stakeholder's situation, scale, and audience are different and can help *catalyze a diversity of momentum*. This will involve urban, rural, and suburban sites. It will involve homes, parks, and farms, and individuals, businesses, and institutions. It is cooperation and collaboration that will galvanize our society for the big shift.

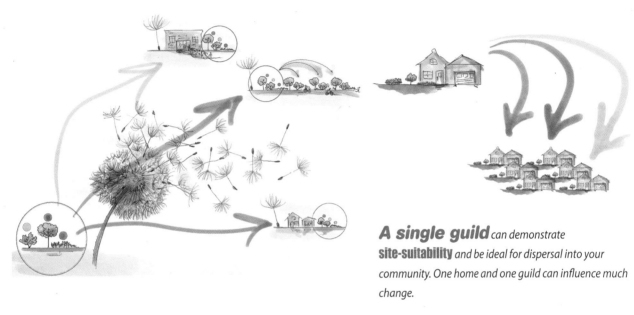

A *single guild* can demonstrate **site-suitability** *and be ideal for dispersal into your community. One home and one guild can influence much change.*

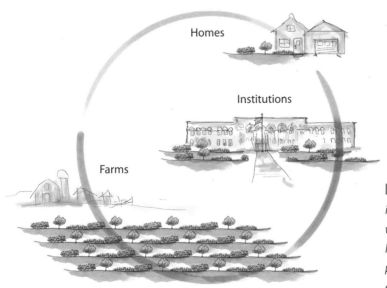

Homes

Institutions

Farms

Multi-stakeholder collaboration *can result in big change as each scale and situation is well suited to different roles. We need living laboratories at homes, education outreach programs at schools, and regenerative ecosystem farming.*

Your home can become an **EPI Site** for spreading change outward into your property, community, and beyond. Small property owners are ideally suited to inspire their communities through edible landscape plantings.

Homeowners can be great **citizen scientists** *when they create site-suitable guild designs. The value of discovering site-suitable plants on a small scale with low risk is immense for larger community spaces where big budgets and public decision-making require sound data.*

Laneways, streets, and other linear spaces can be **transitioned** to edible hedges, which can easily be maintained and enjoyed.

Diseased and dying **monoculture street trees** *can be successioned to provide* **edible ecosystem benefits** *through a diverse understory design. Their energy can be returned to the new understory as freshly mulched beds inoculated with edible, medicinal, and useful fungi and other soil life that feed off chipped wood and decomposition.*

Edible hedge design is a simple patterning of trees, bushes, and ground-covers. **Patterning** can include fruit, pollinator habitat, and nitrogen-fixing legumes.

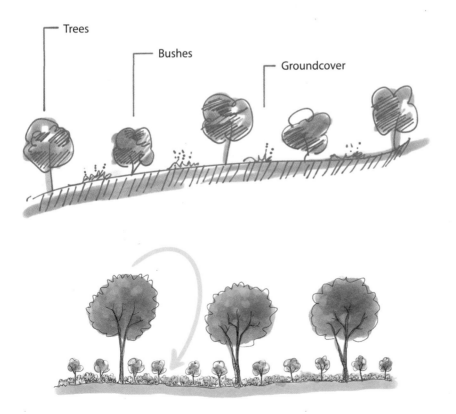

Bike lanes are great sites for **ecological healthcare**. They provide space for recreation, which can be enhanced through the sensational benefits of ecosystem smells, sounds, sights, and certainly, a nutritious snack.

Bike lanes and walking paths can uniquely bridge the spaces between us so that we can rekindle the art of **community well-being**.

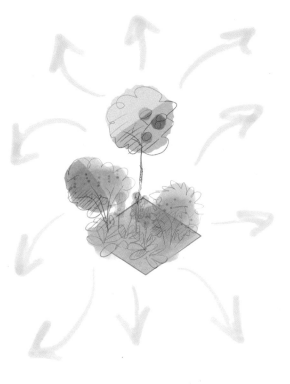

Linear park spaces *in Stockholm's historic Kungsholmen neighborhood are ripe for the inclusion of* **eco-educational panels** *about Sweden's food history and* **ecological healthcare**.

Neighborhoods are the **epicenters of societal resilience**. By orienting our neighborhoods around **accessibility** to necessary resources, we can create truly livable communities that are **more secure in** the face of **socio-economic and environmental change**.

At this scale, we can identify potential **underutilized greenspaces, discover heritage "mother trees,"** and **build core groups**. Mother trees* are those worth spreading their seeds and scions because they show site-suitability.

* Mother trees are those wonderful old growth edible giants we can find in our communities that, If "site-suitable," are ready to disperse their progeny through seeds, suckers, and scions.

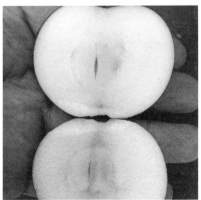

Above left to right: This beautiful cherry tree is mature, disease-free, and high yielding. It is ready to be used for education, be propagated, and inspire community land transition. Societal resilience will come through **genetic conservation, evolution, and dispersal.**

Left: This apple was picked from a mature apple tree found in an Ontario neighborhood; the tree had received minimal care and was disease-free, with perfect fruits as evidenced by this cross-section slice showing no internal insect damage. Finding and marking these "mother trees" is part of the new **ecosystem economy.**

*Ancient olive tree at a church in Cyprus. Olives have been an important staple for Mediterranean culture for thousands of years. Today, olives are threatened by a fungal disease spread through the mechanized harvest of hedge-style production for global export. **Mother trees** can help us find disease-resistant varieties and remind us of the heritage of diverse olive groves.*

Homesteads can be powerful movers of plant material. With the extra space and dedication, homesteaders can **propagate** many site-suitable plants and **experiment** with guild design for larger-scale plots.

This home is a 2.8-acre property on the edge of town. Once a farm, this house is now surrounded by a booming suburb. The land has been transitioned to a food forest with over 300 varieties of edible and useful plants; the site educates under the **EPI System***.** *

* Learn more about active EPI sites at www.ecosystemsolutioninstitute.com.

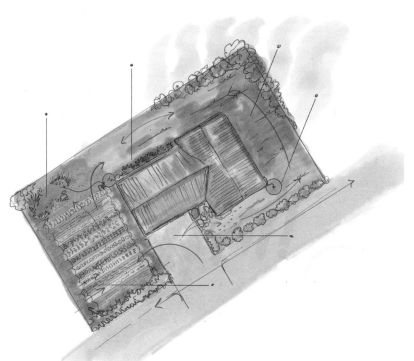

Nurseries and market gardens can be formed from any home or homestead. They have an important role in the preservation of **agrobiodiversity** by making heirloom and endangered food plants available in communities. Many of our heirlooms don't fit in the big agribusiness export marketplace, but their tender and so-delicious skins are just right for fresh sales in our communities.

*Greenhouses, nurseries, and seed companies **are well situated to lead the practice of including long-lasting** **metal labels** **with our food plants. In this way, the site-suitability of successful guilds can be spread far into the future, preserving the** **genetic data** **for posterity and** **facilitating land transition**.*

The **propagation of site-suitable food plants** *needed to transition land is sustained by* active local nurseries, *not big-box stores.*

Schools are the hope of a better society. They can be a grounding point for a **cultural shift** with each generation. Schools, colleges, and universities have the potential to shape their **EPI sites to support curriculum**. Not only will the plants be site-suitable, but signage and information sharing can enrich **outdoor education**.

Educational institutions are great **breeding grounds for change;** they are closely associated with each other through conferences, and students can be the mechanism of dispersal from a school to many neighborhoods. The well-known bake sale could be expanded to include local seed swaps, plant sales, and fresh produce markets. **Ecosystem culture** looks like this—healthy food and sustainable solutions growing from our children's hearts and minds.

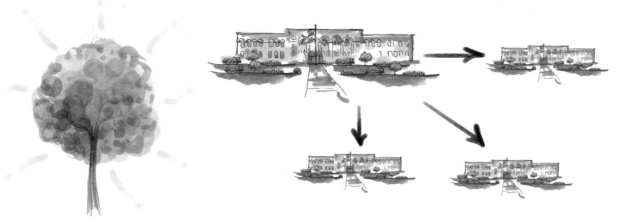

Fruit trees in playgrounds provide dynamic play space, and sources of **fresh snacks, educational opportunities, and shade.**

Outdoor education is critical to changing our communities, and, by exposing society to new ideas and especially our children, we do this generationally. Students at universities and college have opportunities to walk along extensive edible hedges on their way to and from classes in the fall, enjoying berries and discussing exciting ideas.

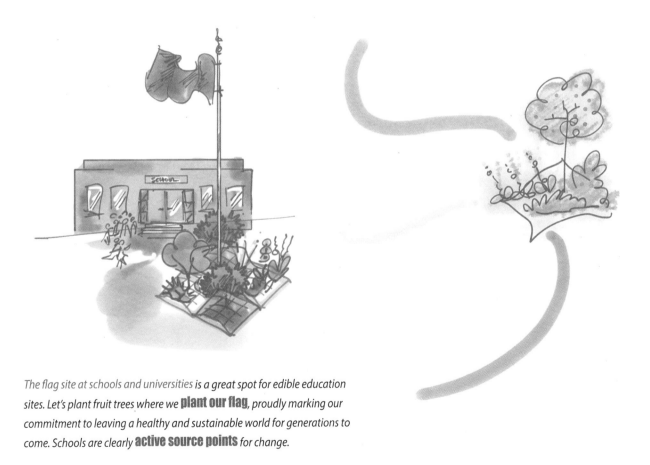

The flag site at schools and universities is a great spot for edible education sites. Let's plant fruit trees where we **plant our flag**, proudly marking our commitment to leaving a healthy and sustainable world for generations to come. Schools are clearly **active source points** for change.

Universities are uniquely suited for deep research and development for **land transition**. They have vast greenspaces for **living laboratories**, and a willing body of students eager to work, learn, and design.

EPI Sites can **integrate the vision and culture of institutions.**

Here, the Kansas City Art Institute can demonstrate the relationships of the "color wheel" to students through a prismatic edible landscape that also nourishes their brains.

Farmers will be major players in meeting the **negative emissions targets** needed to **mitigate climate change**. Ecosystem-style farming practices sequester carbon in trees, crops, and soil and improve soil health for managing droughts and pest epidemics.

Because farmers tend many acres of land, they are important stakeholders for land transition. Farms should integrate **biodiversity for profitability** *through organized* **Permabeds for regenerative productivity.**

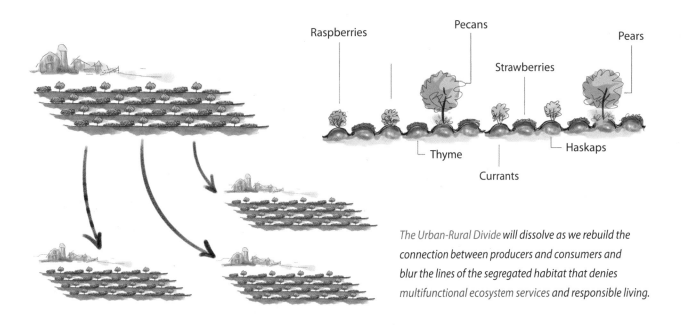

Raspberries
Pecans
Pears
Strawberries
Thyme
Currants
Haskaps

The Urban-Rural Divide will dissolve as we rebuild the connection between producers and consumers and blur the lines of the segregated habitat that denies multifunctional ecosystem services and responsible living.

A practical way of including biodiversity on the farm *is to plant riparian buffers along streams, upland shelter belts along ridges, and* **edible hedges along fences lines***. Among other benefits, they can shelter livestock, reduce stream pollution and farm nutrient losses, and provide additional income sources and economic resilience.*

Edible diversity grown in a farm hedge can include strawberries, haskaps, and walnuts.

Communities will be influential in building **food security**. You cannot depend on food sources from the outside in times of disaster, social upheaval, or technological disruption. Without close-by access to food, many communities could be described as food deserts.

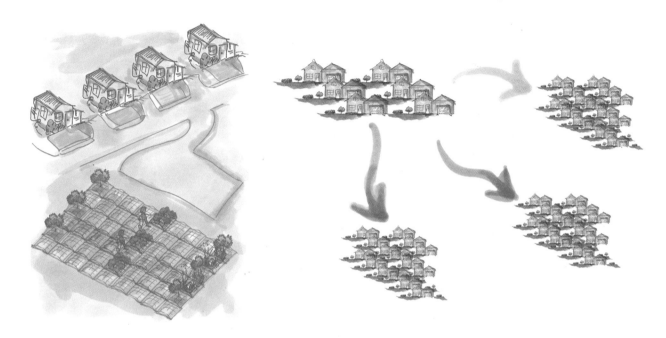

A pillar of food **security** is having **food grown near-to-home**: in your garden, public parks, and urban, suburban, and greenbelt community gardens and farms.

The Seed Bank at the Institute for Meso-American Permaculture is shown on the left. Social media is a powerful ally in bringing education and inspiration to your community—sharing skills, successful designs, and inspiring photos. It is also a great way to network for plant sharing, work bees, and harvest festivals.

Cities will be major players in societal change. Their ability to act as self-governing entities for **big land-use changes** is a key to their potency. For instance, they could implement city-wide plans for edible ecosystem accessibility for citizens. **Policy development grows** on the city level.

Well-known city landmarks are highly visible sites for inspiring and helping to promote change. Those cities that transition will see increases in tourism, property values, and quality of life. The tourism potential for cities is immense. **Earlier adopters** *will be situated on the world stage as truly green cities. Our monuments, museums, and iconic greenspaces are key EPI Sites with* **edible eco-education for shifting society.**

An edible hedge can be anywhere. We can **leverage culturally significant land-scapes** to promote change. Take, for instance, this beautiful edible hedge. Consider its power for change when located across from the architecturally beautiful "painted lady" houses in San Francisco. Would they be as beautiful if they weren't painted? Consider what it means to go without something. Once we have fruiting communities, would we choose to go without?

Tourism in such famous places can promote ecological landscape change for homes across the nation.

Regional influence can be powerful. Once entire regions transition to edible ecosystems, from town to town and city to city, farm to farm, the land between will change due to natural and human dispersal. **As the land changes, people will change, and our culture will transform.**

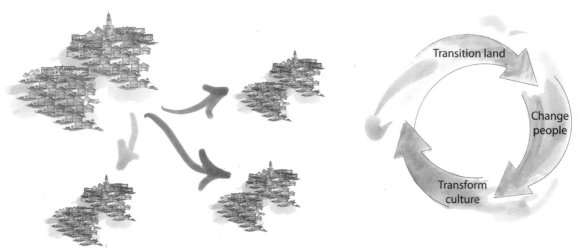

Regions should be tackling broad land-use issues and maximizing EPI sites to solve and encourage the changes we need to see through **land planning, management, and policy.**

Regional land transition can encourage **best management practices** that could rehabilitate eroding traditional grazing lands on the Mongolian Steppes. **A cultural shift** needs to occur **for stewardship to be sustained.** Changes in the land will prove the value of stewardship as profitable practices and community well-being are enhanced. The **impact of restoration** upon climate change will be a global cherry on top of the pie of regional wealth and resilience.

The Great Wall of China is visited by over 10 million tourists per year. As the only manmade object visible from space, perhaps it could serve as a superb educational opportunity for **global cultural transformation,** *and, with 1.4 billion people, China could be a leader in* **edible ecosystem design.**

Leadership

Zoom out to see a multi-national viewpoint. *Consider the partnerships and* **leadership** *that is arising. Spot-by-spot we take our land in hand and make big changes bit by bit. Leaders will emerge within communities, and political leadership will be positioned to influence greater regional change with key EPI sites.*

Who will be the leaders to make edible diversity a priority? Who will make ecosystem services integral to our cultural landscape? Decisions and policy-making should be grounded in societal success, community well-being, and profitability through regenerative economies.

There are opportunities everywhere, and highly visited public places are ideal for engaging citizens. These key EPI sites will build momentum for national and regional changes.

Food security leadership is needed. Food security is a critical issue in **northern** and remote communities. Accessibility to fresh fruit and vegetables comes at great cost. EPI sites in **remote communities** can highlight the potential for suitable food plants.

A feasibility design of the Yukon Archives highlights the landscape potential for food security education at the Yukon University, which is now celebrating the launch of the Yukon University, the first Arctic university in Canada.

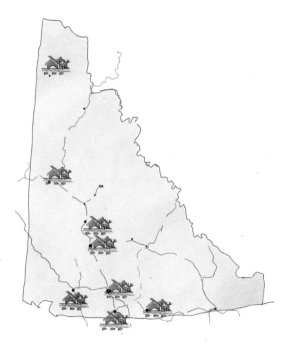

Above is shown an EPI site conceptualization for Yukon University, Canada. The work, being done by the Klondike Valley Nursery near Dawson City, Yukon, is informing other growers and homeowners in the region about the food-plant potential in their area. This progress could be furthered through the EPI System to engage other stakeholders, such as the Yukon University and First Nations cultural centers, for additional EPI dispersal.

Regenerative
Wealth Security

We continue to zoom out and see our Earth with it's rich biodiversity worthy of active conservation through regenerative use.

Our ***regenerative wealth*** must be taken in hand and secured close-to-home in our spots of land! Every biome has wild food ecosystems, heirloom varieties, and landrace **genetics to conserve** and keep alive through conservation, local food production, and **living laboratories**. We are **securing** the foundation of our **societal wealth** in many edible diversity hot spots by putting the power of food and our heritage in the hands of the many.

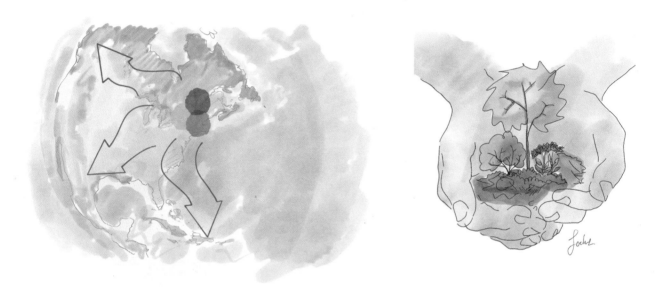

The biological diversity of any region is ***the right of the people*** living there and should be wild in all our yards, building more diversity and securing this wealth for the future.

Every biome should be managed for biodiversity hotspots and include both wild and landscaped ecosystems. Every country has unique ecosystem guilds that are site-suitable to **Earth's different environments.** These can be shared across similar biomes to help inform change between countries with similar environmental constraints.

Our biome is our habitat, and its **ecosystems' goods and services** *are sustained by genetic diversity conservation and evolution. Our minds, bodies, and nervous systems depend on this biodiversity for health and well-being.*

San Francisco could be a **"hot spot" for fruit forest design** *and dispersal of ideas into wine country.*

Vineyards everywhere are **transition-ready spaces** *that are already organized and underutilized; these could be managed for increased profits, sustainability, and community well-being through diversification of land use.*

Countries in similar biomes can **transition together** into edible eco-system abundance. They can also **cooperate and collaborate** for global ecosystem services by leading regional **decision-making** through **cross-pollination** of ideas, strategies, and designs.

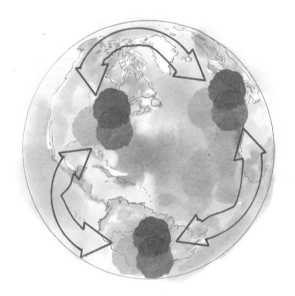

Global change *will happen simultaneously; at every scale,* **leaders** *need to be oriented around food and societal success.*

We need a **global biodiversity farms race**. *How much land can we transition to edible ecosystem design? Our agricultural land is the largest space in need of regenerative management, and the opportunity there is immense. Monoculture land use will dwindle as we design profitability and ecosystem benefits into our foodscape.*

Sister Cities in similar biomes can influence each other's decision-making by **sharing information** on ecological land management for national and international benefit. The ecosystems of Europe, for instance, are similar to those in North America. Ottawa and Stockholm could be sister cities; the two locations have **similar plant hardiness** requirements and overall ecological constraints.

There are many opportunities for land transition and education in the greenspaces overlooked by the Canadian parliament building. The Stockholm city hall also has many **greenspace opportunities**. Similar plants could be grown in both places.

Habitat Is a
Human Right

At last, we have zoomed back out to a global view point, to where this book began, to where our journey started as humans. This is our Earth! But now, through your actions, with our feet planted in our yards, and parks, and farms, it has become diverse, abundant, and edible. It is a true human habitat. And, is this not a human right?

Habitat Is a Human Right

Edible ecosystems, biodiversity, our human habitat— it is a human right—and a challenge—to pick up and plant! The benefits of edible ecosystem culture are apparent; they are ready to be grasped. Who will be there to meet the need for transition—this capability for cultural transformation? Which individuals will stand up? Which communities will gather their local plant resources and trial their potential? Which cities will maximize their greenspaces for edible diverse abundance? Plant a tree. Plant a park! Plant a waterfront… Plant your yards, your community centers, your new developments, your future! **Plant an edible diverse and abundant habitat around us all!**

These spots are points of **conservation and conversation**, places of ethics and activism, and spaces of sanctuary and healing. Each one is a bit of ecosystem that can stand tall in the face of the degradation of our *wild ancestral landscapes* and uphold the resilience of our society in these uncertain times.

Community well being

Biodiversity resilience

Nontoxic environment

Equitable ecological footprint

Ecosystem services

Food security

HUMAN RIGHTS

A new, one-of-a-kind, human rights museum in Winnipeg *could be an EPI site to help this growing city meet the One Million Tree Challenge through* **dispersing inspiration, education, and plants** *that are diverse, edible, and useful; this living museum could help replace the failing elm tree canopy through the EPI System.*

Australia has some of **the greatest diversity** *loss and some of the most vulnerable endemic species.*

Sydney can take a stand in its greenspaces to **adopt the EPI System** *as a framework for influencing land transition and cultural values.* **Return diversity to the people** *as the right to fresh food and a healthy environment to live in.*

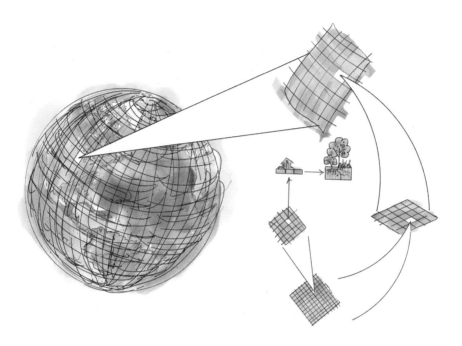

By considering our original nature and the opportunities of our cultural landscape we can see the shortest road ahead to societal wealth, well-being, and resilience. In towns, countryside and cities, we can design and build The Edible Ecosystem Solution: the transition of land to biodiversity and the transformation of culture, one spot at a time, by anyone, anywhere.

One spot at a time, we can reclaim Earth's land as a mosaic of edible ecological homes, parks, farms, and schools. How much of the world is just lawn? How many greenspaces are underutilized and inefficient? How many people would benefit from more edible and useful biodiversity around them?

If everyone on Earth planted one edible ecosystem garden on their own land or within their community, we would have 7.7 billion spots. To compensate for those who do not have the time, money, or space to plant on their own, those with additional means could provide sponsorships. This would be a community-based, multi-stakeholder approach to reclaiming healthy habitat for us all. And, that would be 7.7 billion **source points** for further land transition. If each point influenced three more spots through dispersal of education, propagation, and inspiration, we would have over 23 billion spots. That is 23 billion **living laboratories** working on site-suitable solutions for regenerative land use.

Double that from the natural excitement and inspiration that emerges and double it again, and we would have 92 billion spots! That is 92 billion **edible diversity hot spots** conserving our food heritage and the genetic solutions to our current and unknown problems. These spots amount to *215,000 square kilometers*. This is roughly the amount of land in turf grass in the entire United States. This would be 215,000 km² worth of additional ecosystem services near-to-home.

With this momentum we could transition a significant portion of Earth's *104 million km²* of habitable land to biodiversity for maximum ecosystem services. Global stewardship can conserve endangered ecosystem services, rebuild food sovereignty and security, and ensure a complete transition to world-wide human habitat. What is more, we would have changed people, transformed our culture, and reached a tipping point to an ecosystem world with all its inherent benefits.

By considering our original nature and the opportunities of our cultural landscape, we can see the shortest road ahead to societal wealth, well-being, and resilience through biodiversity. In towns, countrysides, and cities, we find that effective design, many micro-landscapes, and the sum of our stewardship, is *The Edible Ecosystem Solution*: the transition of land and the transformation of culture, one spot at a time, by anyone, anywhere. Remember, to get going: On a journey of a thousand steps, we need plant just one tree. If that is all you do, do it well; do it for yourself, your family, the land, and for posterity.

Get Going Here!

www.ecosystemsolutioninstitute.com

The Ecosystem Solution Institute is dedicated to transitioning landscape to biodiversity through education, propagation, and inspiration.

Endnotes

Section 1

1. Brendan B. Larsen et al., "Inordinate Fondness Multiplied and Redistributed: The Number of Species on Earth and the New Pie of Life," *The Quarterly Review of Biology* 92, no. 3, 2017, https://www.journals.uchicago.edu/doi/10.1086/693564.
2. Eva Crane, *The World History of Beekeeping and Honey Hunting.* Routledge, 1999.
3. Qing Li, *The Japanese Art and Science of Shinrin-Yoku Forest Bathing: How Trees Can Help You Find Health and Happiness.* Viking, 2018.
4. Marilyn Hair and Jon Sharpe, "Fast Facts About: The Human Microbiome," Center for Ecogenetics & Environmental Health, University of Washington, accessed October 26, 2019, https://depts.washington.edu/ceeh/downloads/FF_Microbiome.pdf.
5. Ibid.
6. Theodore Roosevelt, speech before the Colorado Live Stock Association, Denver, Colorado, August 19, 1910.
7. Jared Diamond, *Collapse: How Societies Choose to Fail or Succeed.* Viking Press, 2005.
8. G. Tyler Miller and Scott Spoolman, *Essentials of Ecology.* Cengage Learning, 7th edition, 2014.
9. Jennie Moore, Meidad Kissinger, and William E. Rees, "An urban metabolism and ecological footprint assessment of Metro Vancouver," *Journal of Environmental Management* 124 (July 2016): 51–61, https://doi.org/10.1016/j.jenvman.2013.03.009.
10. Ibid.
11. Gary Haq and Anne Owen, *Green Streets: The Neighbourhood Carbon Footprint of York.* Stockholm Environment Institute, 2009.
12. Global Footprint Network, Advancing the Science of Sustainability website, accessed September 2019, https://www.footprintnetwork.org/.
13. Alexandra Touzeau et al., "Diet of ancient Egyptians inferred from stable isotope systematics," *Science* 46, (June 2014); 114–124, https://doi.org/10.1016/j.jas.2014.03.005.
14. Giuseppe Barbera et al. (editors), *The Wild Apple Forests of the Tien Shan.* Fondazione Benetton Studi Ricerche, Treviso, 2016.
15. "Global fruit production in 2017, by variety (in million metric tons)," accessed August 2019, https://www.statista.com/statistics/264001/worldwide-production-of-fruit-by-variety/.
16. Einkorn.com: Restoring Ancient Einkorn Farro, accessed July 2019, http://einkorn.com.

17. Fred Kabotie and Fred Geary, artwork painted on level two of the Desert Watchtower in Arizona.
18. F.H. King, *Farmers of Forty Centuries: Organic Farming in China, Korea, and Japan.* Dover, 2004.
19. Winnipeg Trails Association website, accessed August 2019, http://www.winnipegtrails.ca/

Section 2

1. Aldo Leopold, *A Sand County Almanac: With Essays on Conservation from Round River.* Ballantine Books, Reprint edition, 1986.
2. E.O. Wilson, *The Social Conquest of Earth.* Liveright, 2013.
3. Tim Benton, Juliet Vickery, and Jeremy Wilson, "Farmland biodiversity: Is habitat heterogeneity a key?" *Trends in Ecology and Evolution* 18:4 (April 2003): 182–188, https://doi.org/10.1016/S0169-5347(03)00011-9.
4. E.O. Wilson, quoted on AZ Quotes website. Accessed October 2019, https://www.azquotes.com/quote/556856.
5. Gerardo Ceballos et al., "Accelerated modern human-induced species losses: Entering the sixth mass extinction," *Science Advances* 1, no. 5 (June 2015), https://doi.org/10.1126/sciadv.1400253.
6. "Smithsonian Tropical Research Institute Panama," accessed August 2019, stri-sites.si.edu/sites/rainforest/diversity_and_survival.html.
7. Chelsea Harvey, "2017 Was a Really Bad Year for Tropical Forests," scientific american.com, June 28, 2018.
8. Global Forest Watch, "Forest Monitoring Designed for Action," globalforest watch.org.
9. FAO, "What Is Happening to Agrobiodiversity?" accessed August 2019, fao.org/3/y5609e/y5609e02.htm.
10. John Horvat II, "How We Went from 17,000 to 15 Main Varieties of Apples," The American TFP, accessed September 2019, https://www.tfp.org/went-17000-15-main-varieties-apples/.
11. "World Population Review," accessed June 2019, http://www.worldpopulation review.com/world-cities/.
12. Philip Ronald, "Options for Shade Tree Diversity in Winnipeg," Jeffries Nursery, 2018, http://www.jeffriesnurseries.com/mbgrow_18.pdf.
13. Manitoba Sustainable Development Peatlands and Forestry Branch, "Five-Year Report on the Status of Forestry, April 2011–March 2016," accessed October 2019, https://www.gov.mb.ca/sd/pubs/forest_lands/5yr_report.pdf.
14. "Pollinators Need You. You Need Pollinators," Pollinator Partnership website, accessed August 2019, https://pollinator.org/pollinators.
15. "The TreeSpirit Project: A Celebration of Our Interdependence with Nature," accessed October 2019, https://treespiritproject.com.
16. Mark L. Heiman and Frank L. Greenway, "A healthy gastrointestinal microbiome is dependent on dietary diversity," *Molecular Metabolism* May 2016, 317–320, doi:10/1016/j.molmet.2016.02.005.
17. Marilyn Hair and Jon Sharpe, "Fast Facts About the Human Microbiome," Center for Ecogenetics & Environmental Health, accessed October 26, 2019, https://depts.washington.edu/ceeh/downloads/FF_Microbiome.pdf.

18. Jianghong Liu and Gary Lewis, "Environmental Toxicity and Poor Cognitive Outcomes in Children and Adults," *J Environ Health* 76(6), Jan–Feb 2014, 130–138, https://www.ncbi.nlm.nih.gov/pmc/articles/PMC4247328/.

19. Shinrin yoku website, accessed October 2019, http://www.shinrin-yoku.org/shinrin-yoku.html.

20. John Muir, *The Mountains of California.* New York: The Century Co., 1894. https://www.loc.gov/item/rc01000874/.

21. Florence Williams, *The Nature Fix: Why Nature Makes Us Happier, Healthier, and More Creative.* W.W. Norton, 2017.

22. Henry David Thoreau, *Thoreau on Nature: Sage Words on Finding Harmony with the Natural World.* Skyhorse Publishing, 2015.

23. Cristina Milesi et al., "A Strategy for Mapping and Modeling the Ecological Effects of US Lawns," International Society for Photogrammetry and Remote Sensing, symposium paper, March 14–16, 2005, accessed on August 2019, http://www.isprs.org/proceedings/XXXVI/8-W27/milesi.pdf.

24. Ted Steinberg, *American Green: The Obsessive Quest for the Perfect Lawn.* New York: W.W. Norton, 2006.

Section 4

1. Daniel J. Bussey, *Illustrated History of Apples in the United States and Canada.* JAK KAW Press, 2016.

2. Julie Sardos et al., "Banana Collecting Mission in the Autonomous Region of Bougainville (AROB), Papua New Guinea," accessed October 2019, http://www.musalit.org/seeMore.php?id=17005.

3. Archimedes (translated by Sir Thomas Heath), *The Works of Archimedes.* Dover, 2002.

Section 5

1. Stephen C. Farber, Robert Costanza, and Matthew A. Wilson, "Economic and ecological concepts for valuing ecosystem services," Special Issue: The Dynamics and Value of Ecosystem Services: Integrating Economic and Ecological Perspectives, *Ecological Economics* 41 (202) 375–392, 2002.

2. Adam Smith, *The Theory of Moral Sentiments.* Penguin Classics, January 2010.

Each spot counts and each is a point of inspiration, education, and propagation to change our world.

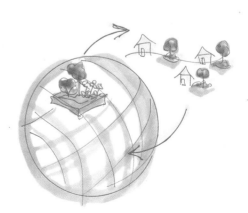

Index

About the Author

Zach is an educator, designer, and grower who specializes in Edible Ecosystem Design through landscaping and education. He consults widely with homes, farms, colleges, schools, and municipalities across Canada and the United States, and through many biomes, from Guatemala and South Africa to the Yukon and Mongolia.

Zach manages an award-winning farm with diversified food forest products, heirloom garlic, and a hardy tree nursery. His innovations have won three provincial awards and are featured in his first book: *The Permaculture Market Garden*.

Zach is the director of the Ecosystem Solution Institute, which is dedicated to the education, propagation, and inspiration of ecosystem solutions for land-use transition. The Institute oversees pathbreaking education sites, including an Edible Biodiversity Conservation Area near Ottawa, Ontario, and a suburban food forest in Winnipeg, Manitoba. Zach is passionate about how small actions—strategically linked—can make big change. His inspiring and empowering vision is presented in his latest book: *The Edible Ecosystem Solution*. For more about his work, please visit www.zachloeks.com

Every step in life is an opportunity to leave the ground beneath our feet more edible and biodiverse. From our backyards to beyond, we can choose our habitat by planting even a few of our footprints into trees, bushes, and herbs.

A Note about the Publisher

NEW SOCIETY PUBLISHERS is an activist, solutions-oriented publisher focused on publishing books for a world of change. Our books offer tips, tools, and insights from leading experts in sustainable building, homesteading, climate change, environment, conscientious commerce, renewable energy, and more — positive solutions for troubled times.

We're proud to hold to the highest environmental and social standards of any publisher in North America. When you buy New Society books, you are part of the solution!

- We print all our books in North America, never overseas
- All our books are printed on **100% post-consumer recycled paper,** processed chlorine free, with low-VOC vegetable-based inks (since 2002)
- Our corporate structure is an innovative employee shareholder agreement, so we're one-third employee-owned (since 2015)
- We're carbon-neutral (since 2006)
- We're certified as a B Corporation (since 2016)

At New Society Publishers, we care deeply about *what* we publish — but also about *how* we do business.

Download our catalogue at https://newsociety.com/Our-Catalog, or for a printed copy please email info@newsocietypub.com or call 1-800-567-6772 ext 111.

ENVIRONMENTAL BENEFITS STATEMENT

New Society Publishers saved the following resources by printing the pages of this book on chlorine free paper made with 100% post-consumer waste.

TREES	WATER	ENERGY	SOLID WASTE	GREENHOUSE GASES
70	**5,600**	**29**	**240**	**30,100**
FULLY GROWN	GALLONS	MILLION BTUs	POUNDS	POUNDS

Environmental impact estimates were made using the Environmental Paper Network Paper Calculator 4.0. For more information visit www.papercalculator.org.